"THERE'S A SUCKER
MINUTE—AND ONE T

Money miracle man Michael Milken—who took in *over 550 million dollars a year* before he ended in prison and his employers in bankruptcy court

Author Clifford Irving—whose "autobiography" of Howard Hughes won him fortune and infamy

The Williamsons—a clan of swindlers who preyed on America for generations

Ferdinand DeMara, Jr.—the "Great Impostor," who brilliantly played roles that ranged from a skilled surgeon to a prison warden

Dorothy Mae Woods—queen of welfare fraud, who lived in lavish luxury while collecting a fortune from California social services

Salvation salesman Jimmy Swaggart—whose lust for loot was bettered by his other lusts

These are but a few of the captivating con artists who did their mind-boggling best to prove that honesty is not the best policy.

GREAT HOAXES, SWINDLES, SCANDALS, CONS, STINGS, AND SCAMS

GREAT HOAXES, SWINDLES, SCANDALS, CONS, STINGS, AND SCAMS

Joyce Madison

A SIGNET BOOK

SIGNET
Published by the Penguin Group
Penguin Books USA Inc., 375 Hudson Street,
New York, New York 10014, U.S.A.
Penguin Books Ltd, 27 Wrights Lane,
London W8 5TZ, England
Penguin Books Australia Ltd, Ringwood,
Victoria, Australia
Penguin Books Canada Ltd, 10 Alcorn Avenue,
Toronto, Ontario, Canada M4V 3B2
Penguin Books (N.Z.) Ltd, 182–190 Wairau Road,
Auckland 10, New Zealand

Penguin Books Ltd, Registered Offices:
Harmondsworth, Middlesex, England

First published by Signet, an imprint of New American Library,
a division of Penguin Books USA Inc.

First Printing, August, 1992
10 9 8 7 6 5 4 3 2 1

PRINTED IN THE UNITED STATES OF AMERICA

To my father, Arthur C. Jenkins—the most honest-to-a-fault person I know—and his wife, Carol Brice Jenkins, librarian extraordinaire. With all my love.

Contents

Acknowledgments

My most sincere appreciation and thanks to:

Madeleine Morel, a literary agent whose patience goes far beyond her abilities, which are great;

John Silbersack, one talented and patient editor;

Jeremy Boraine, a most perceptive and delightful editor; and "The Pink Tea."

Genius accompanies, like a shadow, the tread of the dark, imposturous character of the dedicated impostor.

—St. Clair McKelway
The Big Little Man from Brooklyn

Defining Terms

Bunco (from Italian, "bank," gambling, circa 1872) *n*—a swindling game or scheme.

Con (1889) abbreviation of *confidence*; (1896) *n*—a confidence game; *v*—to swindle, persuade, cajole.

Fraud (from 14th-century Latin) *n*—deceit, trickery, intentional perversion of truth in order to induce another to part with something of value or to surrender legal rights; an act of deceiving or misrepresenting; impostor, cheat, one who is not who that person pretends to be; something that is not what it appears to be.

Hoax (probable contraction of *hocus*, circa 1796) *n*—an act intended to trick or dupe; something accepted or established by fraud or fabrication; *v*—to trick into believing or accepting as genuine something false and often preposterous.

Scam (American slang, 1965) *n*—a fraudulent or deceptive act or operation.

Sting n—an elaborate confidence game; *v*—to overcharge or cheat.

Swindle (from Old English, coined circa 1782, "to vanish") *v*—to take money or property by fraud or deceit.

Introduction

People are endlessly fascinated by imaginative swindles and scams—the more elaborate or outrageous, the better. We often experience a perverse joy in hearing about a person or a situation being exploited through sheer cunning and connivance, our appreciation of a well-run scam dictated by its colorfulness or complexity.

Slick con artists pulling off adventurous swindles may fire our imagination and feed our desire to get even with the system, change identities, or tell that big lie. We tend to admire the fearlessness of an imposture well done, and some of us even wish for the requisite chuzpah and acting ability to execute the perfect hoax.

While swindlers and scam artists break the law, how they break the law sets them apart. They appear audacious, bold, daring, often reckless—everything most of us would love to be but are too law-abiding or rut-oriented to even try. Some people even perceive the ingenuity used to create a magnificent hoax, scam, or con as bordering on brilliance, and many an imposter is categorized as a genius.

Con artists—unless cruel or vicious—can seem inherently romantic: we are captivated by the cleverness of their scheme, and sometimes even disappointed at their ultimate downfall. Unless they rip off the elderly of life savings or steal funds from widows with children, we smile and nod and almost admire the culprits and their entertaining antics.

Whether motivated by greed, a desire for power and fame, or by the sheer pleasure of accomplishment, con artists, swindlers, and imposters operate with apparent shrewdness; after all, to keep from getting caught, they must stay several steps ahead of their victims. Their knowledge of human behavior, body language, and people's weaknesses—along with their desire to deceive and their facility for exploiting others while ingratiating themselves—sets these brazen individuals apart.

We may end up despising the more unscrupulous tricksters, but their agile imaginations and often unorthodox schemes make for entertaining reading; many of the boldest have proudly written autobiographies—either before, during, or after prison.

The challenge—the excitement and everpresent danger of being exposed—proves most appealing to frauds, impostors, and con artists; treading the straight-and-narrow would imprison them far more than any jail. Were these glorified deceivers and cheats to aim their usually high intelligence in honest directions, experts say their potential for success could be almost limitless.

Motion pictures, television, and literature are full of unconventional heroes whose incredible con games all but boggle the mind: Newman and Redford in the Oscar-winning *The Sting*; George C. Scott in *The Flim Flam Man*; James Garner and Louis Gossett, Jr., in *The Skin Game*; James Coburn in *Dead Heat on a Merry-Go-Round* and *Harry in Your Pocket*; Ryan and Tatum O'Neal in *Paper Moon*; Joe Mantegna in *House of Games*; Tony Curtis in *The Great Impostor*; Steve Martin and Michael Caine in *Dirty Rotten Scoundrels*; and most recently, Anjelica Huston in *The Grifters*; as well as TV's *Switch* with Eddie Albert and Robert Wagner, *Colonel Flack* with Alan Mowbray, *The Rogues* with Charles Boyer and David Niven, *Ten Speed and Brown Shoe* with Jeff Goldblum and Ben Vereen, and *P.S. I Luv U* with Connie Sellecca and Earl Holliman. Audiences never seem to tire of the inventiveness of confidence tricksters.

In literature, probably the most renowned con artist is Leslie Charteris's debonair Simon Templar in the mystery story exploits of the Saint. Considered the Robin Hood of modern crime, the Saint outcons the con artists in book after book, film after film. The Saint has been played in movies by Louis Hayward, Hugh Sinclair, and George Sanders, and in 114 TV episodes by a pre-007 Roger Moore. Another literary con artist was E.W. Hornung's Raffles, the Amateur Cracksman.

In real life, the best scams and hoaxes never come to light. In motion pictures, *The Sting* offers a prime example of this—if the victim becomes aware of a swindle, the con is a bust. For a sting to be successful, the victim must never know he or she has been had. Of course, also in real life, many swindled people feel too humiliated or embarrassed to come forward and report a crime once they realize they've been had.

Great Hoaxes, Swindles, Scandals, Cons, Stings, and Scams profiles the most flagrant, sensational, and remarkable swindlers and impostors of recent years. This entertaining book contains the crème de la crime of the world's greatest grifters, along with the most fascinating hoaxes ever executed.

Included are such amusing tales as how author Clifford Irving actually got away with the publishing world's scam of the century, only to outsmart himself by confessing his deed when he mistakenly thought he'd been caught out; how twenty-four people created a bestselling novel in less than two weeks, complete with fake author and rave reviews; how the Pasadena welfare queen took the government for the biggest financial ride in U.S. history but tripped herself up by being too greedy; how one man married and ripped off over 105 women but was caught by the wrath of a woman scorned; how a woman pretending to be a man fooled and humiliated nearly all of Mexico City's most prominent leaders and took the secret to her grave; how an attorney who wanted to make a name for himself faked out the scientific world for nearly two decades; how the city of San Francisco perpetrated a hoax on itself; and how people can protect themselves from the con artists' most recent scams.

Because of the constant innovations and new twists on old schemes, by all rights, *Great Hoaxes, Swindles, Scandals, Cons, Stings, and Scams* should be published in a three-ring binder to accommodate updates and inserts as con artists and hoaxers come up with newer and better ideas, twisting the old ploys to fit the times. So prolific are the tricksters, and so eager are they to get their hands into other people's pockets, it would be fair to assume that the number of new swindles and hoaxes executed before this book hits the stands will match the number included herein.

Someone once said that no one can con a truly honest person, since it takes a certain amount of avarice or dishonesty on the victim's part for a flimflammer to pull off a good scam. As long as greedy suckers look to get rich quick or expect something for nothing, there will be grifters and con artists eager to take advantage of them.

Spokespersons for most local bunco squads emphasize: Beware! If something looks too good to be true—it probably is!

CHAPTER 1

Artistic Scams

Genius on Canvas

ELMYR De HORY, considered the greatest art forger of the twentieth century, faked well over $60 million worth of almost undetectable Impressionist, Post-Impressionist, and French Fauve paintings. The flamboyant Hungarian refugee, who posed as an international art collector, could turn out a Matisse, Modigliani, Picasso, Renoir—or any other twentieth-century master—at a moment's notice wherever he happened to be. When he needed the cash, he'd create a "master" in his hotel room or at a friend's home, manipulating even the most sparse supplies into a masterpiece.

To explain his vast and apparently endless art collection, the exotic Hungarian known as Elmyr Dory-Boutin claimed to be of royal lineage. He told everyone he had inherited a large royal-family fortune, including innumerable priceless paintings smuggled out of postwar Hungary. With his ability to duplicate the style of any artist, he produced "new" paintings no one ever questioned. If the art dealers who sold his "collection" for him piece by piece ever suspected anything, they never called attention to it. On the other hand, the dealers De Hory went through could never be accused of being overly honest.

De Hory made his home on the Spanish island of Ibiza, southwest of Majorca, where he enjoyed the company of other artistic people from many different countries. Included in the artists' colony was De Hory's close friend and neighbor, the relatively unknown American author, Clifford Irving.

Irving had had a few unremarkable books published by McGraw-Hill in the United States, and he convinced De Hory to permit him to write a biography of the painter, *Fake!*, which told the world the artistic genius's true story. The author assured the art forger that the world would finally acknowledge De Hory's work and buy originals from him.

When Clifford Irving's book came out, De Hory and his friends feared possible legal problems from the Spanish government—with an incumbent prison term—because of De Hory's admitted forgeries. Instead, local officials pounced on him, and he spent two months in an Ibiza jail, convicted not of art forgery or fraud, but of homosexuality and consorting with known criminals (the art dealers who peddled his fantastic fakes). Meanwhile, Irving's book on De Hory proved to be a momentary bestseller.

The Howard Hughes Con

CLIFFORD IRVING, obscure novelist and author of an exposé of master art forger Elmry De Hory—*Fake!*—finally made an international name for himself in the literary world—but not quite the way he had originally intended. In 1971, having been a trusted but less than spectacular author for twelve years with McGraw-Hill Publishing—the world's largest publisher—and on the heels of his somewhat critically successful book, *Fake!*, Irving set about concocting one of the most cleverly convoluted scams in literary history. The then forty-year-old writer hoodwinked his trusting publishers and *Life* magazine of nearly $1 million, created more notoriety and uproar than Taylor and Burton, and landed himself in federal prison.

Not considered a very good writer, unimaginative at best and a hack at worst, Clifford Irving found himself in the eye of a media tempest when he faked a Howard Hughes autobiography purportedly "dictated to me alone." The eccentric billionaire's predictable and expected denial of the document's authenticity only served to diminish everyone's doubts.

Irving didn't just decide one day to pull off

the literary hoax of the century and rip off his publishers for millions of dollars. But with the unknowing assistance of an extremely private recluse whose closest employees were confused and battling one another, and a public clamoring for anything and everything about Howard Hughes, the stage was set—with Irving in the starring role, prepared to upstage the title character.

In 1970, when Howard Hughes applied for a gaming license as he began to buy into the Las Vegas gambling world, the Nevada gaming commission demanded the billionaire's presence at the gaming-license hearing. Apparently in one of his more utterly reclusive periods, however, Hughes refused to show. Two of his top men spoke for him, each claiming to be Hughes's only authorized spokesperson and denying the other's validity.

When Hughes sent a handwritten letter to clarify matters, the commission first questioned the authenticity of the handwriting and then accepted it. The media grabbed the front-page story and had a field day, gaining great mileage from the reticient billionaire's strange behavior and reclusive ways.

A sample of Hughes's handwriting spread from continent to continent: *Newsweek* printed a photograph of the last few lines of the handwritten document. *Life* followed with a full-color photocopy of the entire letter.

When the magazines reached the artists' colony on Ibiza off the south coast of Spain, Clifford Irving and his artistic friends saw the opportunity for a scam too delicious to pass up. No one had seen Howard Hughes for several years, and obviously the eccentric billionaire refused to even come out of seclusion long enough to save his holdings in Las Vegas. Some speculated that Hughes had gone completely mad; others said the sixty-five-year-old might actually be dead, while his henchmen "kept him alive."

Irving reasoned that if the media and the gaming commission couldn't pry Hughes out of his shell, and the public devoured every available morsel of news about the peculiar billionaire, how would the world react to his denial of an autobiography? The time was right, the world was ripe, and Clifford Irving was ready, along with his buddies, to pluck the million-dollar plum.

While he practiced forging the billionaire's handwriting, Irving quietly approached his editor at McGraw-Hill. He claimed that, after sending Hughes a copy of *Fake!*, he had been contacted by Howard Hughes himself, who was so impressed with the tactful and understanding way Irving had treated De Hory's unusual life story, that he wanted Irving to do the same for him. The writer produced a handwritten letter in which Hughes purportedly explained his reason for choosing Irving as his biographer. Part of the letter was later used in the book's advance press release, stating that Hughes chose Irving because of his "sympathy, discernment, discretion and integrity as a human being."

Irving faked one letter after another from Hughes, his forgery abilities growing with each letter, and showed his editors three handwritten letters allegedly from the billionaire to prove what he said. McGraw-Hill executives, recognizing a potential goldmine and knowing a hot property when they saw one, offered Hughes a $500,000 advance against royalties—through the recluse's established biographer and go-between, Clifford Irving.

Documents and contracts shuttled back and forth, with Hughes's signature finally sealing the deal. Above and beyond the project's obligatory total secrecy, the eccentric one demanded a major stipulation that at first seemed a little odd to the publishers—he preferred his royalty-advance checks, after the first installment, be made out to H. R. Hughes and given to Clifford Irving, who was to receive half the advance. A simple request easily accomplished. By this time, the McGraw-Hill executives would probably have agreed to almost any request.

Of course, Irving relied heavily on the secrecy "requirement," which no one at McGraw-Hill questioned. "Hughes" insisted that, if one word about his autobiography got out before the book went to press, the deal would be off and he could keep whatever monies had been paid him. Less than a handful of McGraw-Hill people knew who "H. Octavio" on the contract really was. Time, Inc., bought serialization rights for $250,000 and agreed to the same payments and secrecy as the publisher.

Irving then created tales of clandestine meetings with Hughes, protracted phone calls, more secret get-togethers—over one hundred sessions in "various motel rooms and parked cars throughout the Western Hemisphere," from Mexico to the Caribbean, the Bahamas, and everywhere in between. The writer claimed the two worked together on the manuscript but that the billionaire actually dictated everything into a tape recorder and then read over the final draft after it had been transcribed.

Before the work was completed, however, the situation changed. Hughes, Irving explained to his publisher, decided he wanted to do an autobiography—as told to Clifford Irving. The writer would act as editor on the billionaire's work, and the entire work would be in Q&A form, with Irving asking the questions and Hughes answering them honestly.

Irving's editors were thrilled when the writer produced the first pages, but everyone at McGraw-Hill and Time-Life who knew of the project remained leery, considering the eccentric Hughes's history of abruptly changing his mind and reneging on deals. In fact, they proposed the unusual arrangements for payment of the advance against royalties because of the billionaire's quixotic behavior.

As it stood, McGraw-Hill would pay only $100,000 upon signing of the contract; then another $100,000 upon completion of the research; and the final $300,000 upon receipt of the manuscript. Clifford Irving knew his scam had hit paydirt—his publishers never doubted him for a minute. They focused all their wariness on the eccentric Hughes and took the innocuous Irving for granted.

As the work rushed toward completion, Irving told the publishers that a snag had come up—one that might have ruined any other writer's deal: Hughes, Irving claimed with a straight face, had decided that his autobiography was worth more than a mere half-mil. In fact, Irving, in a moment of greed and with the project going so well, had decided to go for broke and up the ante.

Before showing the publishers a letter he had "received" in which Hughes insisted that if McGraw-Hill didn't increase the advance against royalties to $850,000 the billionaire wanted Irving to take the manuscript to another publisher, Irving explained that Hughes had originally demanded a full $1 million for his autobiography. Irving told the publishers that—with McGraw-Hill's best interests at heart—he had talked the billionaire down $150,000 to $850,000.

Irving waved a check from Hughes for $100,000 drawn on a Swiss bank—the amount of the original advance—which the letter instructed Irving to return to the publishers if they turned down the new offer.

Clifford Irving took a big chance by bringing his faked letter and check to McGraw-Hill, because his entire scheme could all fall apart if someone challenged him. But no one dared—too much at stake. Instead, after much discussion and with the publishers' relief, the writer offered to take a recommendation of $750,000 to Hughes, which, of course, his imaginary "partner" would accept.

The publishers, realizing any house in the country would all but kill for a Howard Hughes autobiography, eagerly agreed to the change in the contract. When the work was done, there would be 230,000 words in hardcover, which should sell out several editions right from the start. *Life*, holding serial rights, was ready to publish the book in three installments.

Irving knew cashing checks made out to H. R. Hughes would be difficult, so he planned well ahead. The only person he knew who spoke German fluently and would not be noticed or questioned about financial transactions with a Swiss bank when depositing or withdrawing money from a Swiss bank was his wife, Edith. She practiced signing H. R. Hughes, and a fake passport under the name of Helga R. Hughes made the scam package complete—Edith would deposit and withdraw money from a Swiss account under the name H. R. Hughes.

Edith Irving went to Zurich and opened an account under Helga R. Hughes, using the first advance check from McGraw-Hill for $100,000 made out to H. R. Hughes. A couple of days later, she withdrew most of the money and opened an account at a different bank across the street from the first, thus laundering the money to cool down the trail. She repeated the process with each advance check.

Not only did the real Howard Hughes and the entire Hughes Tool Company blast McGraw-Hill and Time, Inc., when the publishers jointly announced to the media that an autobiography would be forthcoming shortly, but the Hughes attorneys attacked, gaining an injunction against the book's publication. Thus the swindle began to unravel stitch by stitch.

Everyone in on the scam felt that, while Edith Irving represented the sting's weakest link, aside from coaching her and keeping an extremely close eye on her, their hands seemed tied and very little could be done about it. To their amazement, however, when the world's greatest literary swindle began to unravel, Clifford Irving himself proved to be the weakest link of all.

Under such pressure when the district attorney questioned him, Irving assumed the authorities knew more than they did, and he panicked. Not knowing that his freedom was just moments away because no one could prove who "Helga" was, Irving opened his mouth and stuck both feet in. In a frantic effort to get the pain of his questioning over with quickly, he blurted out that Edith was Helga. At that point, the previously hamstrung DA placed Irving under arrest and wrapped up his case. Had Irving kept quiet and said nothing about Helga/Edith, he and his buddies would have remained at large—a million dollars richer.

The New York district attorney who set up the verbal sting was fortunate that Clifford Irving fell for his scam. The literary con artist, along with all his artistic friends, ultimately became a "folk hero" who wound up in federal prison. The clever web Irving wove almost worked; and his hoax and its final outcome are better than any fiction piece. A number of people got a great deal of mileage from it.

As a postscript, Clifford Irving served his prison term and upon his release went right back to authoring books, his name much more recognizable for having pulled off such a scam.

Bestseller by Committee

In the late 1960s, Long Island's *Newsday* reporter MIKE McGRADY came to the conclusion that "bad writing is being rewarded—as long as it's sexy enough and has enough violence. Just look at Harold Robbins and Irving Wallace!" From this assessment came the germ of a brainstorm that would lead to one of the greatest hoaxes in the modern literary world.

McGrady felt sure anyone—with or without talent—could turn out the junk the public bought and devoured like so much movie popcorn, and he set out to prove his point. He tacked a note to the *Newsday* bulletin board, asking for writers to create a sleazy novel in one week's time. His premise was, if enough people each wrote one chapter, an entire novel would result in no time.

McGrady wanted the contributors to write "sexy and bad," so his only rules were: 1) there must be an unremitting emphasis on sex; 2) true excellence in writing will be quickly blue-penciled into oblivion. The storyline: Jillian Blake, demure Long Island housewife with six kids, exacts revenge on her cheating husband by sleeping with every man in the neighborhood. For consistency's sake, through October, she could be described as being well tanned. From November 15 on, she had alabaster flesh.

Twenty-four *Newsday* reporters and editors—including two women and two Pulitzer Prize winners—volunteered to grind out a chapter each. Reporter John Cummings did his in four hours over a six-pack of beer. In a little over one week, everyone completed their assignments, and a sleazy novel was born. It took Mike McGrady and Harvey Aronson another eighteen months to whip the material into shape for submission.

While the reporters smoothed out the writing and connected all the disjointed chapters, they also searched for a title and an "author" for the book—someone who would front the novel and go on interviews if necessary. They already had a pen name befitting a romance writer: Penelope Ashe. After quite a hunt, they finally came up with McGrady's sister-in-law, Billie Young. She seemed perfect—she looked the part of a housewife romance writer, and she was willing to go along with the hoax.

They rehearsed her until she could answer their questions as if she actually had written the book. In practice, the reporters asked the fake Penelope what virginity meant to her. She batted long lashes and replied, "Virginity is like a Tiffany lamp—fragile and from another era." Just the right amount of sincerity.

A committee came up with the ultimate title: *Naked Came the Stranger*. That said it all.

McGrady brought the completed package to Bernie Bookbinder of the prestigious Lyle Stuart publishing house and explained what he had in mind. Rather than trying to bamboozle the publisher, he hoped Bookbinder would buy it knowing it was a deception. If the novel sold well, admitting the hoax later would help sell additional copies; if the novel bombed, nothing was lost.

McGrady and his *Newsday* reporters found the right publisher in Bernie Bookbinder. A man with a good sense of humor and a true sense of adventure, Bookbinder went along with the hoax. The rest is history—*Naked Came the Stranger* sold well over one million copies in sixteen languages and earned over $250,000 back in 1969. The novel stayed on the bestseller list (fourth, below *The Godfather* by Mario Puzo, *The Love Machine* by Jacqueline Susann, and *Portnoy's Complaint* by Philip Roth, and just above *The Andromeda Strain* by Michael Crichton).

Critics raved about the novel, and Penelope Ashe made the rounds of all the TV and radio talkshows. Kramer of the *Long Island Press* opined, "Penelope Ashe's scorching novel makes *Portnoy's Complaint* and *Valley of the Dolls* read like *Rebecca of Sunnybrook Farm*."

Dell published the paperback version, and an X-rated movie tried to do the novel justice. Each of the twenty-four creators, and Billie Young, received $5,000 along with their moment of glory on the *David Frost Show* when they announced to the world what they had done. Rather than hurting the book's sales, this picaresque revelation actually boosted them.

The Hitler Diaries Scam

Documents dealer KONRAD KUJAU took *Stern*, the flamboyant West German photojournal magazine, for $3.8 million, allegedly with the assistance of the magazine's crack investigative reporter Gerd "The Detective" Heidemann. The flashy German publication, which prided itself on presenting material to its readers long before any other periodical could, bombastically boasted an exclusives policy of "Everything money can buy!"

Under normal circumstances, the staff of such a freewheeling magazine willing to do anything for a scoop would never have been hoodwinked by such an elaborate and expensive hoax; because of the amounts of money offered for inside information, the checks installed in the editorial infrastructure to protect the journal and its publisher, Gruner & Jahr, against fraudulent stories were normally almost failsafe. The special situation surrounding this unique case cried out for the ultimate in secrecy, however, and precluded the proper precautions that would otherwise have protected *Stern* from the 1983 swindle that rocked its very foundations and nearly toppled it.

In 1983, Heidemann came to his editor, Thomas Walde, with the incredible news that someone had contacted him, claiming to have discovered a stash of twenty-seven diaries kept by Adolf Hitler. Personal diaries in the führer's own handwriting—private thoughts, unguarded emotions, rigorous reminders.

Heidemann told his editor that, from what he'd been told, the journals had been among Hitler's personal effects flown out of Berlin as the city fell in the waning days of the European front of World War II. According to Heidemann's sources, the plane carrying the diaries was shot down near Dresden, but farmers salvaged what they could from the wreckage and cached it away for safekeeping. The investigative reporter explained that his sources just recently came across the material.

After Walde gave the investigative reporter the go-ahead, obtaining the journals wasn't easy—Heidemann animatedly described such cloak-and-dagger exploits as furtive meetings with East German generals and former Nazi officers, bribes to high government officials, the heaving of bundles of cash from the open window of one moving vehicle to another on the autobahn—covert exchanges for the diaries, one batch at a time. All could have been lifted straight from an espionage novel by John le Carré or Andrew Kaplan.

A select few at *Stern* and Gruner & Jahr met for secret "reading sessions" in which they voraciously ripped through each newly arrived bundle of the black, cheap imitation-leather-bound journals, devouring the contents. The personal entries dated back as far as 1932 and continued right up to shortly before D-day. In fact, the last entry appeared almost as if an adolescent female had written it: "Dear Diary—Must close now. Bormann wants all my documents to be sent away."

To ensure secrecy, the magazine kept the number of people privy to the existence of the diaries down to a bare minimum—Heidemann's immediate superior, Walde, who circumvented protocol and went over everyone's heads to the assistant director of the publishing firm and to one member of the board. All plans for publication of the diaries in their entirety went through four men only.

Shortly before publication, Gruner & Jahr quietly sold the foreign syndication rights to Rupert Murdoch's *Sunday Times* in London, *Paris Match*, and Italy's *Panorama*. After intense negotiations with *Newsweek* in this country, Gruner & Jahr allowed the American publication to pass up the offer of serialization rights but gave them permission to print the story of the diaries' existence as a cover article after the fact.

As news of the impending publication hit the media, a number of historians pointed out that Hitler preferred to dictate his thoughts to someone else rather than write them down himself. Still other experts noted that, in the last years of the war, Hitler suffered from a debilitating palsy that would have drastically distorted the legibility of his handwriting. When it was disclosed that even the most recent diaries showed none of the trembling the beleaguered war leader had displayed, warning bells went off at Gruner & Jahr—and around the world.

Finally, upon testing the diaries' paper—the first step critics insist should have been taken—any number of postwar materials, including polyester fibers, showed up in the chemical analysis. Now, in hindsight, many of the entries seemed almost laughable: "Must not forget to get tickets for the Olympic Games for Eva Braun."

In another entry, Hitler delights in receiving congratulations from one of his generals on his "fifty years of military service," which would have been politically expedient except that Hitler was at that time only forty-eight years old. The diaries were littered with anachronisms, errors, and figments of the forger's own imagination. And all eyes turned to those four men who had kept the secret and worked on the project in private. Why had such experienced men not questioned the authenticity of the documents?

Everyone with anything to do with the diaries, and especially Heidemann, left the publication or was fired. But when admitted perpetrator Konrad Kujau faced charges of forgery and fraud, he pointed an accusatory finger at Gerd Heidemann and insisted the investigative reporter had been in on the scheme from the start and had even dictated some of the entries. Heidemann denied the allegations.

Don't Let the Truth Get in the Way

JANET COOKE, eager young reporter for the *Washington Post*, received a Pulitzer Prize for journalism in 1981. She had discovered a homeless waif, a hopeless drug addict who would do anything for a fix. The youngster's photograph—splashed from coast to coast—made Cooke a hero. Her story about this pathetic young fellow tugged at the nation's heartstrings and brought her to the attention of the world. Cooke came to the public's attention once again when her story was proved a total fabrication.

Cooke indeed had found rampant squalor and drug addiction in young children on the streets, but her story proved to be a composite of several youngsters. By focusing on just one little boy, she evoked more pathos than had she told the truth, but she ruined her reputation and her career.

Janet Cooke was stripped of her honor and labeled a fake. By stretching the truth to the point of fraud, and getting caught at it, the investigative reporter lost her award, her job, and her reputation. Had she pointed out that her story was fiction or a composite, she might have won an award for her sensational writing—and she might still be writing for the *Washington Post.*

Pre-Animal Rights Get-Rich-Quick Scheme

Most hoaxes are based on someone's sense of humor. A classic hoax from a kinder, gentler time took place in 1904, when a coal mine collapsed in Harwick, Pennsylvania, near Pittsburgh. Richard J. Beamish of the Philadelphia *North American* reported in his lead on the mine disaster: "God sits on the mountains of Harwick tonight while, below in the valley, Death and Sorrow lurk."

Tradition has it that the newspaper's night editor wired back to the reporter: "See God. Get Interview. Rush picture."

In another classic hoax, the Washington, D.C. National Press Club's publication, *Goldfish Bowl*, in 1940 exposed an 1875 hoax that would have sent shock waves throughout the land had it been perpetrated today. Of course, no one would have thought to try it today, and no one would have been able to get away with it, had it been tried. But in 1875, a quieter and more gullible time, life was easier and people believed everything they read and heard.

In 1875, the Associated Press ran as fact a story supplied them by editor Willis B. Powell of Lacon, Illinois. Powell's "news" ran in most newspapers across the country, and his hoax made quite a hit. Powell claimed to have received a prospectus offering a method of becoming enormously wealthy almost overnight. Touted as a foolproof scheme, investors could make unbelievable amounts of money through very little effort in even less time and at almost no overhead.

Most newspapers carried the prospectus almost verbatim, explaining that a "glorious opportunity" was opening up whereby a company would be pioneering a "cat ranch." (Don't try to add up the figures—it won't work!) Starting with 100,000 cats, each of which should give birth to an average of 12 kittens per year, the number of cats would multiply rapidly. Each cat's skin, when ready for market, would sell for 30 cents.

With only 100 men to skin 5,000 cats per day, there would be a net daily profit of $10,000. As to what to feed the cats while waiting to be skinned—rats would be ideal. To that end, a rat ranch would be set up next door to the cat ranch, and 1,000,000 rats would be raised. Because the rats breed twelve times faster than the cats, there would be four times as many rats to feed as cats.

Food for the rats, of course, would prove no problem at all, because the rats could be fed the carcasses of the skinned cats. The prospectus pointed out that with the rats from the rat ranch acting as food for the cats, and the skinned-cat carcasses from the cat ranch going as food for the rats, the cat skins would virtually cost nothing to obtain.

Although this kind of naive hoax might have gone over back in 1875—and was not exposed until 1940—contempory animal-rights groups would have stormed the Capitol steps had this article appeared as a news item today.

Trouble in River City

WILLARD TALBOT, a modern-day Professor Harold Hill, tore a page right out of the Broadway musical comedy *The Music Man* as he blew through one town after another in the mid-1960s, selling a $489 package of cheap musical instruments to children. Just as in the Broadway musical, the kids' instruments came with free music lessons, guaranteed to have the youngsters playing to performance capacity in time to march in the New Year's Day parade at the Rose Bowl in Pasadena, California.

Lured by the jovial con artist's seductive sales pitch, doting mothers and fathers found it difficult to turn down an opportunity for their children to participate in such a prestigious event. More than four thousand parents bought the package.

If it was too late in the year to reasonably prepare the children for New Year's Day, Talbot promised the budding musicians their own Rose Bowl concert, topping the original musical comedy's fraudulent claim. Of course, Talbot followed in the footsteps of his "mentor" and beat it out of town before either the parents or their offspring realized they had purchased nothing more than inferior musical instruments and pie in the sky over Pasadena.

That Synching Feeling

With dreadlocks bouncing and elbows jouncing, ROB PILATUS and FABRICE MORVAN danced and pranced their way across the music video stage to the driving beat of "Girl You Know It's True." Better known as Milli Vanilli, the two handsome young black performers spoke with German accents and danced with artistic enthusiasm as they "sang" in harmony and enchanted the world with their music.

The year 1989 was all Milli Vanilli's—their debut album for Arista Records went platinum and they received the music world's highest recognition, the Grammy award as best new artist 1989. The world seemed at their feet as the pair of music-video superstars catapulted into the rarefied stratosphere of the few whose work sold more than six million copies.

But they had barely received all the money and fame when the walls of their dreamworld crashed in on them. As the news broke that Morvan and Pilatus had sung not one note of the album that brought them their success, the very people who had embraced them now turned on them. Before the feathers settled, the Grammy had been returned and Milli Vanilli had been disbanded. In a world where lip-synching has been a necessity for some, getting caught at it is the ultimate crime and carries with it the ultimate price.

Dishonesty Is Its Own Reward

DAVID BEGELMAN, president of Columbia Pictures, embezzled from his own company by writing small ($10,000) checks made out to movie stars and cashing them himself by forging the star's name. In a community where checks for such paltry amounts usually go unnoticed, Begelman could pad his already sizable paycheck with impunity. In the 1980s he took Hollywood and Wall Street and might never have been caught were it not for an innocent victim who blew the whistle and nearly ended his own career.

Oscar-winning actor Cliff Robertson noticed he had been "paid" $10,000 by Columbia Pictures but had not worked for them in the year the check was written. The IRS wanted to know why he had not declared the $10,000 earnings, and he decided to look into the situation. With the IRS breathing down his neck, Robertson asked Columbia's accountants for the canceled check, which they produced. He pointed out that the signature on the back was not his.

When it came out that Begelman had been busy with some creative bookkeeping, Robertson called foul, since the actor felt he should not have to pay tax on "income" he had never earned nor received. When interviewed, Robertson came off as unjustly used, because he was innocent of any wrongdoing. On the *Phil Donahue Show*, he said, "We're trying to stop a corruption that has become malignant in our industry and grown every year."

Unfortunately for Robertson, Hollywood all

but embraced the culprit and turned its back on the whistle-blowing victim. While many outside the industry felt Begelman had acted heinously and should pay for his crimes, citizens of Glitzburg, USA, merely grinned and clucked their creative tongues at the "naughty boy" in their midst. Instead of doing hard time in prison for the felony grand theft he was found guilty of, Begelman received a Tinseltown slap on the wrist in the form of a $5,000 fine and three years probation doing public service. A year later, after Begelman produced a film on the dangers of the drug PCP, Burbank Municipal Judge Thomas C. Murphy—who had originally sentenced the embezzler—reduced the man's conviction from felony to misdemeanor, then changed Begelman's plea to not guilty of the lesser charge and revoked the remaining two years probation, saying, "He can go forward without the stigma of probation."

As the deputy district attorney sputtered, and Cliff Robertson and others stood by in amazement, Begelman returned to head up Columbia Pictures—before being named president of Metro-Goldwyn-Mayer. In fact, the *Los Angeles Herald-Examiner* ran a headline: BEGELMAN'S BACK AND MGM'S GOT HIM. And while Begelman flourished, Cliff Robertson found himself out of work and nearly unemployable. Over fifteen years went by before someone had the nerve to cast the actor in a significant role.

In David Begelman's case, crime does pay—just ask Cliff Robertson.

CHAPTER 2

Hilarious Hoaxes

San Francisco's Prank

EMPEROR NORTON I, "Emperor of the United States and Protector of Mexico," started out as financier Joshua A. Norton. In 1849, the young magnate arrived in San Francisco from Algoa Bay, Cape of Good Hope, with a bankroll of over $40,000 from various trading ventures in Africa and South America. He planned to build a vast financial empire in this burgeoning new country and by 1854 had amassed nearly $250,000, a mind-boggling fortune in those days—more than enough capital to keep even the worst spendthrift in luxury for several lifetimes.

Norton, on a roll and in a flamboyant speculation, boldly invested *every penny* he possessed in rice, confident he could corner the market by buying up all the rice in California. Under normal circumstances, this daring move would have ensured his place in economic history as one of the wealthiest men in the world. Everyone west of the Rockies would have to come to him for rice.

Unfortunately for the young capitalist, ruin in the shape of three ships from the Orient, holds bulging with rice, came sailing through the Golden Gate.

Norton was bankrupt. Stunned and penniless, his promising future and fortune scuttled, he disappeared from public view for nearly five years. He was soon forgotten, and history has no record of how Norton spent those five destitute years.

One day in 1859, however, Joshua Norton appeared at the *San Francisco Bulletin* office with a "proclamation" to be printed from "Emperor Norton I." Because he was dressed in pseudomilitary garb and seemed quite serious about his outrageous edict, the editor printed it—as a joke. But the people of San Francisco were not only amused, they were touched by the proclamation and accepted Norton as their emperor, thus beginning a poignant and harmless hoax perpetrated by an entire city on itself.

Ignoring the fact that Norton had probably lost all contact with reality, his subjects treated him royally. A local printer made up Emperor Norton currency for Norton's own personal use, and it was accepted everywhere. Restaurants, bars, all public places, took his paper money in lieu of cash or gold dust—for his use only, of course.

Usually dining in a different establishment for each meal, Norton became the city's recognized connoisseur. If he became displeased with a restaurant, he let his feelings be known—and business dropped off dramatically. The eateries he regularly patronized all proudly displayed signs in their windows declaring Emperor Norton Eats Here and did a brisk business.

While every major city—and even some smaller municipalities—had their own town characters, Emperor Norton became an institution in California. Steamship lines gave him free passage, and the Southern Pacific Railroad issued him a lifetime pass with full dining-car privileges. San Francisco picked up the tab for repairing and replacing his garish uniforms. The Presidio, a U.S. fort, allowed Norton to review the troops; and the University of California, across the bay in Berkeley, welcomed his review of their cadets. Norton attended every session of the state legislature in Sacramento—and was even allowed to make suggestions from the floor.

The ersatz emperor also had his own permanently reserved seats for opening night at the theater—front-row center of the balcony—for himself and his two ugly stray dogs, Bummer and Lazarus! And when he and his royal mutts entered the theater, the audience would rise from their seats and stand in respect.

While many laughed convulsively and then ignored as pure madness Emperor Norton's endless recommendations to improve the city and the state, those who were still alive years later would see his prophetic ideas acted upon: Just as Norton advised, the swamplands east of Montgomery Street were filled in so more land would be available for additional buildings; a bridge would go up to span the Golden Gate, and another would make the East Bay accessible. Buildings were razed so some streets could be widened to permit a heavier flow of traffic; streets were paved, and gaslights were put up so decent women were safe to go out at night. But at the time he proposed all this, many people sneered at its impossibility and his obvious lunacy.

Emperor Norton even proclaimed December 25 a state holiday for children and ordered his subjects to erect and light a gigantic Christmas tree in Union Square. This they did, and to this day, a giant Christmas tree is decorated and lighted in Union Square each holiday season.

Emperor Norton the First reigned for over twenty years, beloved by his subjects. And when he died in 1880, he was accorded the finest funeral San Francisco had ever seen, paid for by the elite Pacific Union Club, a private men's club. In all sincerity, flags flew at half-staff, and thirty thousand mourners attended Norton's funeral. To this day, his likeness is included in the Wells Fargo museum of San Francisco history, and his story is told in history books. What started out as a humorous hoax ended up as a way of life—and one of the most delightful and heartwarming pages of San Francisco's history.

The World's Greatest Impostor

FERDINAND WALDO DeMARA, JR., known the world over as the Great Impostor, is just that—probably the greatest impostor of all time. Some called him a genius and—considering the number of variety of positions he undertook and held capably without being caught—he probably was. Lacking the necessary education or background experience for any of the situations he accepted, DeMara posed and worked competently as a state prison warden, a college dean of philosophy, and a naval surgeon.

When finally caught out, DeMara had assumed the identity of Joseph C. Cyr, M.D., of Grand Falls, New Brunswick, Canada. In 1952, during the Korean War, the thirty-year-old DeMara—without benefit of a high school, let alone, medical school education—performed heroic combat surgery as Dr. Cyr, made headlines around the world, and found himself in prison for impersonating several members of the U.S. armed forces—all AWOL at the time.

Never one to profit from his impostures, DeMara seemed to delight in taking on someone else's name and profession and living as that person. With no formal education, he taught college classes in psychology as Robert Linton French, Ph.D.; he worked in zoology as biologist Cecil Boyce Hamann, Ph.D.; and enrolled as a law student, lived as a Trappist monk, enlisted as an American sailor and soldier, and worked as a hospital orderly and a deputy sheriff—among other positions and endeavors. And his surgical exploits in South Korea were described as brilliant.

DeMara's beginnings in Lawrence, Kansas, appear quite unspectacular. Raised Catholic, he ran away from home at age sixteen and joined the Cistercian monks in Rhode Island. During his varied life of impostures, he tended to return to the cloth with frequency. A delightful personality and a gift for learning helped DeMara create so many personae that Hollywood made a film on his life—starring Tony Curtis as the affable DeMara.

When asked why he did what he did, DeMara answered, "I guess I've always wanted short cuts. And being an impostor is a tough habit to break." He felt his unusual way of life stemmed from "unbridled ambition redeemed by the drive to do good."

Hollywood's Nobility

PRINCE MICHAEL ROMANOFF, one of the world's most engaging impostors, took on his persona of Russian nobility to erase his ignoble beginnings rather than to defraud. Born Harry Gerguson in Brooklyn in 1890, he ultimately became one of Hollywood's darlings. At first storming the movie industry like anyone else, trying desperately to be noticed and cast in films, he got nowhere.

Not until he found a "hook" did he make headway with the right people. Posing as a Russian prince—who purportedly renounced his "title" in 1958—the man known as Michael Romanoff hosted a posh Beverly Hills restaurant, Romanoff's, which many people believed was his. The man's flamboyant portrayal of the thickly accented, snobbish restaurant maitre d' brought him notice and offers of small parts in films. He later acted in motion pictures, typecast as a Russian nobleman or a maitre d'.

In the 1950s, being seen at Romanoff's was the equivalent of dining at Spago in the 1990s. While his restaurant's closest competition came from another celebrity haunt, Chasen's, Romanoff's offered royalty and that certain European charm.

While most people in the showbiz industry realized Romanoff was nothing more than a delightful fake—an engaging front—they played along with his ruse, since it hurt no one. The playful Hollywood crowd found it great fun to rub shoulders with royalty, even if only make-believe. But since Hollywood makes its livelihood from make-believe, Mike Romanoff fit right in, phony Russian accent and all.

The Mysterious J. Fortescue

Few in the scientific community of the 1920s and 1930s wondered why the renowned San Diegan J. Fortescue failed to attend the banquet in his honor or to personally accept the $10,000 Fleischmann prize awarded him for clinical achievements in his research of yeast. Everyone knew the president of the International Board of Hygiene and member of the California Mycological [fungi] Society preferred to live a solitary life of experimentation and contribution to scientific journals of the day.

Acknowledged for his contributions to the literature on myriad subjects, including such diverse topics as polio and the sexual habits of the American male, J. Fortescue received a lengthy and lofty biography in the 1936 *Who's*

Who in San Diego and newspapers rushed to report his scientific exploits.

During Prohibition, Fortescue and his cronies traversed the border from San Diego into Mexico strictly for research purposes. In Tijuana, the scientists judged various local beers for diverse qualities, and Fortescue proclaimed one of the *cerbezas* as calorie-free. News spread and San Diego billboards touted the Mexican beer's nonfattening characteristics.

Only a handful of people knew J. Fortescue's secret: The man did not exist; he was the brainstorm of a real scientist, the fun-loving pathologist Rawson Pickard, M.D., of La Jolla, California, and his practical-jokester buddies. The fictitious scientist served as cover for whatever pranks the men delighted in pulling, including starting up the fake International Board of Hygiene as a cover for their mischief. One of Pickard's friends, Clifford Graves, M.D., even wrote up Fortescue and his scientific accomplishments in the *San Diego Medical Society* magazine.

The playful medical men created J. Fortescue in the Tijuana bar the night they declared one Mexican beer calorie-free. The pranksters based their reclusive scientist on the real British jurist, Sir John Fortescue, 1385–1479, who proposed the moral principal still valid today: It is better that the guilty escape than the innocent be punished.

J. Fortescue's recognized scientific career

continued to flourish until shortly after Dr. Pickard's death in 1963. But thirty years' mileage off a single prank concocted during a dry spell is not bad.

Mexico's Raffish Secret

DON CARLOS BALMORI and SEÑORITA CONCEPCIÓN JURADO share a common burial site in Mexico City. Indeed, they died on the same day and at the same time—November 27, 1931—as inseparable in death as in life. The meticulously cared-for gravesite draws tourists and friends; and, to this day, on the anniversary of their demise, a memorial service broadcasts over the leading networks.

Don Carlos could be considered Mexico's twentieth-century equivalent of Don Quixote, and those who met him kept his secret while he lived, cherishing it and him in a bizarre fandango of love and respect. Everyone who knew Don Carlos remembered his words: "Nothing is as it appears to be. Nothing is real. Not even I."

Reportedly the world's wealthiest man, his money was said to have come from holdings in Cuban sugar, Bolivian tin, Chinese opium, and whatever else created an abundance of pesos. Everyone knew the resplendent descendant of pure Spanish forebears lived in a lavish castle outside Mexico City, held enormous estates throughout the country, and vacationed in his fabulous villas on the Riviera and throughout Europe.

Gossip of his lust for the women grew, because everyone acknowledged Don Carlos as the world's greatest lover—with, as rumor had it, at least "fifty" marriages after any number of betrothals. But the woman sharing his final resting place was never either his wife or his mistress.

In fact, Concepción "Conchita" Jurado, daughter of Ignacio Jurado—Don Carlos's gardener—never even made the newspapers until her death. Sixty-seven years old at her death, she is buried with her full-length portrait in tile, a slender woman with steel-rimmed spectacles and graying black hair. She never married.

In explanation of the double burial, one of Mexico's best-kept secrets was an exclusive club where initiation proved costly if amusing. Until Don Carlos's death, no one even made mention of it, although many who belonged were also members of the media who would ordinarily kill for the sort of scoop the club represented, but refrained from even hinting at its existence, publicly or privately.

On a cool autumn night, Señor Rodriguez came as a guest of Don Adolpho to a gathering held in the two small rooms of Don Carlos

Balmori's gardener. At least thirty-five finely attired people crowded into the limited enclosure, their opulent automobiles jamming the driveway and street out front. A festive occasion, everyone enjoyed themselves as the two newest arrivals ventured in on Señor Rodriguez's first visit to one of Don Carlos's unusual, almost campy soirees.

Don Adolpho had agreed to bring his friend, Señor Carlos Arturo Rodriguez, a newspaper magnate, who secretly hoped to interest his host in investing in a new publication. Perhaps this might be the night, Señor Rodriguez prayed, since it was said that the multimillionaire was most receptive to new projects at these weekly gatherings.

With great pomp, Don Carlos, followed by his entourage of secretaries and other attendants, stopped everything to greet the two new arrivals. He took each by the arm and introduced them around the room, chucking the young women under the chin and making no attempt to hide his rakish interest in them.

One of the secretaries whispered loudly into the host's ear that Señor Rodriguez was a publisher and was hoping to start up a new venture.

"Oh, really?" Don Carlos seemed fascinated. "Please tell me of your plans."

All eyes fell on the publisher as he described his plans for a new magazine with worldwide potential. Don Carlos nodded intently.

"That's quite an idea you have there, Señor Rodriguez, and just out of curiosity, how much will you need to finance the project?"

This came too fast for the publisher. He gulped and said, "Well, I could bring it in for less than a half-million pesos."

"No! No self-respecting magazine stays afloat on less than two million pesos funding. As a publisher, you should know you need enough capital to carry the publication for at least one year without added revenue." Don Carlos thought for a moment, and then said, "I would enjoy being a publisher. I will buy half-interest in your proposed publication—for the full two million pesos. You bring the expertise, and I bring the funding."

As the astonished publisher looked on, Don Carlos snapped his fingers and reached for the pen his secretary thrust into his hand. In moments, Señor Rodriguez saw a check for the full amount.

As the publisher reached for the check, Don Carlos yanked it back and said, "Now, my partner, are you a member of the Masons?"

Señor Rodriguez shook his head, puzzled by the strange question. "No, sir, but I am a member of the Lodge of the Moose."

"Oh, yes? Well, tonight you have reason to be proud." He waved the check at the man. "I bet your antlers are mighty and huge. Let us all see just how large your antlers are."

The publisher laughed weakly. "But I am a Moose in name only—it is a brotherhood."

Don Carlos shook his head vehemently. "You are all such liars! You call yourself a moose, but you have no antlers! How can I go into business with someone who has no antlers! Show me your antlers or I'll keep my check!"

Stunned, the publisher raised his arms above his head and waved them frantically.

"A two-legged moose?"

Señor Rodriguez hesitated, then dropped to his knees and tried to crawl on all fours; but he needed his arms to make antlers. Jerking his arms up while crawling on his knees, he attempted to appear as a moose.

The multimillionaire motioned Rodriguez up and extended the check again, then stopped. "That mustache you wear—it is larger than mine! I never do business with anyone whose facial hair outdoes my own."

"But I have had it—"

"No, forget the partnership. I could never abide a man who cannot compromise."

"I'll cut it down, I promise. I have no problem with that. The first thing tomorrow, I will have it trimmed down to half its size."

Don Carlos rocked back on his heels. "Oh, you say that now, but tomorrow you will forget. No, either you do it now, or the deal is off." He pocketed the check with most of it sticking out for all to see.

With a flourish, a secretary produced a pair of cutting shears, and Don Carlos approached the quivering publisher.

"I'll do it myself," Señor Rodriguez pleaded. "If I do it, it will be done to my satisfaction, and then you may have your check."

In moments, the mustache was no more as the publisher's exquisite facial hair fell to the floor—and his face bore only a scrubby bunch of half-inch whiskers.

When the publisher caught sight of a reflection of the mess above his lip, he started to protest; but Don Carlos gave out a cry: "I have been robbed! My diamond tie pin is missing! No one move!" He called for the police, but the chief of police was one of the guests and quickly stepped forward.

All eyes rested on Rodriguez, who understood he was under suspicion and belligerently demanded he be the first to be searched. The publisher's dismay became overpowering as the police chief dipped his hand into the man's pocket and withdrew Don Carlos's pin.

Cries of "Arrest him! Thief!" echoed in the small enclosure.

"Don Carlos! I beg of you," the publisher yelled. "I am no thief!"

The multimillionaire bounded to a chair in the middle of the room and smiled down at the quaking man. "This is true, my dear sir.

You are no thief. Just as Don Carlos Balmori, the renowned Spanish multimillionaire is neither Spanish nor a millioniare. In fact, nor even a man!" With a flourish, off came the hat to reveal long tresses. With a yank, the fake mustache fell to the floor, revealing a lovely older woman.

"In truth, I am Conchita Jurado—daughter of the gardener Ignacio, in whose home you are now—and "sister" of your host. Thank you, Señor Rodriguez, for allowing us an evening of pleasure."

The arrogant, patronizing Señor Rodriguez had just been treated to a *balmoreada*—one of the republic's greatest-kept secrets, where pomposity and vanity met humility, and greater inner understanding prevailed. All this from a young teenage girl who had dressed up one day to impersonate the real Don Carlos Balmori and fooled her parents so well that she continued with the impersonation at most family gatherings. When the real gentleman passed on she was still a teen, his memory lived on through Conchita and her impersonations.

With the aid of friends in the media, a complete biography and history of Balmori grew until "he" became legend, stories of his exploits growing more lavish by the year. By 1925, the famous one attracted great names. Finally, anyone who wanted to take someone down a peg, brought that person to the Jurado household, where the fictitious Balmori delivered a *balmoreada*.

Save Us from Naked Animals!

In the 1950s, ALAN ABEL, a good-hearted prankster, took the media by storm when he demanded in all apparent seriousness that animals be clothed and consequently formed the fictitious Society of Indecency to Naked Animals (SINA). After the *San Francisco Chronicle* ran a series of four serious front-page stories, each with an in-depth interview of SINA's director, Alan Abel, every talkshow in the country picked up on Abel, who became the flavor-of-the-week guest.

The director of SINA made a number of visits to *The Tonight Show*, where Abel insisted people clothe their pets, claiming it to be obscene to view animals without something covering their "parts." Not until after Abel proposed a full line of animal clothing for farm animals as well as house pets did the hoax come out.

On a 1985 *Phil Donahue Show*, Abel set up another situation, in which members of the audience began fainting. After a half-dozen or more fakes hit the floor, Abel announced that he and his group FAINT (Fight Against Idiotic Neurotic TV) wanted to make a statement against poor-quality television.

As recently as January 1990, Abel concocted a hoax in NYC in which he put a young woman up in a Manhattan hotel, where she said she was celebrating having won $35 million lottery. Much of the media picked up on it. If it's off the wall, it's probably a hoax by Abel.

CHAPTER 3

Religious Ripoffs

TV or Not TV—What's Your Suggestion?

"Passing the plate" in church has never been considered begging—it's doing the work of the Lord. With all that temptation of cash in abundance, there are opportunities for fraud and theft—and danger (Jim Jones)—all in the name of religion. Now that television has taken tent preachers about as far as they can go, bunco artists find it all too easy to become wealthy while milking a naive and trusting flock dry.

Collections of cash have always placed temptation in the path of those manning the tollbooth. Religious donations of any amount of cash can lure the collector to the gates of Hell. In fact, within the last few years, vast religious organizations have crumbled through the baseness of their leaders' greed. In a telecommunicative age where unseen viewers fill envelopes with paper money and send them off as love offerings to the televangelist with the smoothest tongue or the most heartrending plea, temptation rears its golden head and bites the hands it feeds.

One "good cause" after another has folded recently from a healthy dose of greed and clerical deceit. Jim Bakker's Pentecostal PTL tumbled before fundamentalist Baptist Jerry Falwell's hostile takeover (one PTL official portrayed Falwell as the T. Boone Pickens of the religious world); and Oral Roberts's claim that God would "take him home" if a financial quota of $8 million weren't met by a specific date—a rash assertion that caught the eye of both financial and religious authorities—nearly scuttled his operation and brought about federal lawsuits.

Pat Robertson's untainted Christian Broadcasting Network nearly went belly-up from everyone else's problems; and Carl Stevens of the Massachusetts-based Bible Speaks Church filed bankruptcy when ordered to give back several millions of dollars a federal judge alleged had been bilked from an unhappy parishioner.

So long as there is the potential of money to be made in such vast quantities as the televangelical world attracts, religious empires will sprout up to pick the fruit of other followers' labor. Temptation steps in and the wrong pockets swell until it becomes so noticeable that the authorities must put a stop to it—and the empire crumbles, just in time to make room for another to set up shop and reap the golden harvest.

Cost of Adultery—Forty-five Years

JIM and TAMMY FAYE BAKKER allegedly blended fraud, sex, and religion for years. Televangelism made them millionaires, and sexual improprieties made them paupers. Jim and Tammy Faye presided over *The PTL Club* TV show in the 1980s, entertaining and entreating their viewers to send in donations. Jim's broad grin and melodramatic manner went well with his clean-cut look. Tammy Faye's heavy-handed use of makeup went along with her slightly off-pitched voice as she sang hymns for the members of the audience. The head of the PTL [Praise the Lord or People That Love, take your pick] televangelistic organization, fortyish Bakker unfortunately ran afoul of his parishioners and the general populace when his sexual peccadilloes went public.

Jessica Hahn, a former PTL secretary, claimed to have been raped and sexually used by the mesmerizing Jim Bakker. John Fletcher, a defrocked and avowedly gay minister—and Bakker's right arm—admitted procuring Jessica Hahn for Bakker as well as enjoying homosexual sex with the televangelist. Fletcher also suggested that a number of PTL staffers engaged in gay cruising within the organization. Author Austin Miles (*Don't Call Me Brother*) claims to have walked in on a naked scene in which a nude Bakker and his equally unclad young male workers romped sexually in the steamroom.

Another PTL employee, Jean Albuquerque, tells of Bakker's "floozie Jaccuzi"—located in the televangelist's office—in which Bakker usually tried to seduce visiting young lovelies—including one Miss America, over whom Bakker and another church officer openly fought to see who would bump her in the bubbles.

From the millions of television viewers the Bakkers pleaded with during each sermon, the PTL took in over $150 million from about 150,000 contributors. Because of all the attention drawn to the adulterous Bakker and his wife-swapping workers and possibly gay staffers, the spotlight also focused on Bakker's influx of funds. The IRS and other governmental agencies looked into the ultimate destination of that revenue, especially the amounts arriving in cash, since Bakker admitted he and his wife had no head for monetary figures—just for spending it.

Tammy Faye proved Jim's point about not understanding finances when, for his birthday, she presented him—on the air during *The PTL Club*—with two live giraffes! The studio audience, rather than reacting negatively to seeing their hard-earned donations going to something as expensive and as frivolous as giraffes, jumped to their feet and applauded her choice of gifts. There is wide speculation that the congregation lived vicariously through Jim and Tammy Faye, and whatever luxuries the Bakkers enjoyed and flaunted gave them pleasure.

In an extremely clever piece about the Bakkers in *People* magazine, writer Dave Barry sums up the phenomenon quite well: "You can't do good unto others unless you feel good about yourself, and you can't feel good about yourself unless you have a lot of neat stuff."

PTL staffers admitted that when they worked in the mailroom, the contents of incoming mail went into two separate piles—cash and checks. The checks were to be deposited in the PTL bank account, while the currency was diverted to "petty cash" and the amount was rarely recorded. Jean Albuquerque alleged tens of thousands of dollars came in as cash and went out as petty cash.

Part of the cash received from PTL members became hush money to bribe Jessica Hahn into keeping silent about Jim Bakker's flings with her; but she talked anyway, and kept right on talking.

When the authorities arrested Bakker and attempted to handcuff him, the televangelist with a history of emotional instability fell to the floor in a fetal position and sobbed. His wife explained that he did this often. Outside, photographers crowded around as the bawling Bakker howled and simpered and pleaded with his captors to let him go as they dragged him to the police vehicle.

At his trial, Bakker again broke down and blubbered so inconsolably that he had to be carried from the courtroom. The bizarre behavior of this once handsome and youthful televangelist led to psychiatric testing as his sanity came into question. But, judged sane, he was forced to go on with the trial.

Jim Bakker, found guilty of 125 federal counts of fraud and embezzlement, received a forty-five-year sentence for having too many fingers in too many financial pies. Tammy Faye planned to wait for her husband, all the while remaining the butt of comics' jokes about her grotesque eye makeup. Her heavily mascaraed false eyelashes have been described by merciless comedians as two tarantulas in heat or, when she cried and liquefied her lashes, as two holes in the side of the *Exxon Valdez*.

As for their future? If the Bakkers have anything to say about it, their gullible TV parishioners will again make them rich. In the meantime, a judge looked into the severity of Jim Bakker's sentence and decided that forty-five years was far too much. Although his sentence has been shortened to eighteen years, Bakker may remain in prison long enough to repent. Tammy Faye's TV broadcasts in Orlando might bring in enough revenue to start up again where he left off—but she now plans to divorce him.

Cry and You Cry Alone

JIMMY SWAGGART—a bombastic Baptist televangelist whose private life unexpectedly became a prime reason for not living in a glass house—pointed a wagging finger at Pentecostals Jim and Tammy Faye Bakker from his TV pulpit and hurled a few moral boulders as he shamed the beleaguered couple for their duplicity and sexploits. How could this pair of trusted televangelists defile their calling and hoodwink their viewers and worshipers? Adulterous sex, homosexual encounters, wife swapping—all sins of the highest order—how could they do it?

In the most reverent tones possible, Swaggart admonished the Bakkers against ever preaching the gospel again. How could such sinners lead an innocent flock? Offering the Bakkers free advice during his televised sermons, the Baptist preacher, his voice trembling with anguish and scorn, demanded that the unworthy PTL leaders step down. Their sins against the flesh were unpardonable. Nothing short of their relinquishing the leadership of the PTL would save them.

In delivering such mediawide rebukes, Swaggart all but toppled his own financial TV goldmine. While Swaggart hid behind the skirts of his own ministry, effecting a holier-than-thou stance so contemptuous that viewers cringed, the world discovered that Swaggart himself had been lifting a few too many streetwalkers' skirts.

As the Bakkers' travails and Swaggart's recriminations splashed across every form of mass communication, saturating the airwaves and the printed page, unexpected complications set in as a result of Swaggart using his TV pulpit to castigate the Bakkers.

Those who study the occult probably nodded wisely and said something about Swaggart's karma, because what the televangelist did to others was bound to come back to him—like the Golden Rule in reverse—what goes around, comes around, with a vengeance. And what might appear to the outside world as petty behavior would seem unforgivably un-Christianlike to those inside the golden circle of the religious community.

Factions wanting to staunch Swaggart's attacks on Bakker found the perfect means—a prostitute, seeing Swaggart during one of his more vicious attacks on the Bakkers, recognized the "pure preacher" as one of her regular clients. Debra Murphree called a news conference and testified that Swaggart hired her to play with herself in front of him—sometimes in his own car—and, finally, to have "a little" sex with him. She also swore that Swaggart asked that her preteen daughter join in on the sexual festivities for a price.

The media's field day with this explosive news eclipsed the Bakker's problems. Debra Murphree, now a major celebrity, joined Jessica Hahn in her tour of the talkshows, bringing Swaggart's sexual problems into almost every living room in the country. Although Swaggart sobbed wretchedly as he prostrated himself before his congregation in a TV apology, the pettiness of his judgmental attitude toward the Bakkers indeed boomeranged on him; and his parishioners questioned his sincerity and honesty.

Preachers crying while apologizing for past sins—or out of religious emotion—became the standard joke on late-night talkshows as one comic after another got mileage out of, first, Bakker's weeping, and then Swaggart's wailing. Finally, it came to light that Bible-thumpers often weep in an attempt to move their congregation to donate more money. Some not as blessed with acting ability as others use a handkerchief soaked with fresh onion juice to evoke the desired tearful "emotion."

Unfortunately for televangelists Bakker and Swaggart, the ongoing scrutiny over their alleged crocodile tears finally attracted federal investigators, and suddenly their past actions became no laughing matter.

Apparently not having learned his lesson the first time around, Jimmy Swaggart made headlines again in October 1991 when the police of a small California town pulled him over for driving on the wrong side of the road—only to find him in the company of another prostitute.

Holy Credibility Gap

Televangelist ORAL ROBERTS—best known for his faith-healing and his Tulsa, Oklahoma–based Oral Roberts Evangelistic Association and Oral Roberts University—shocked the world when he announced that he needed $8 million fast or the Lord would "call him home." Not once, but twice, Roberts told his parishioners that the Lord would take him if he didn't bring in enough donations.

Akin to crying "wolf!," this may have been seen as a ploy to rake in the gold by more than just the televangelic-weary world. Donations dropped, and it appeared that Oral Roberts would soon be called "home." Instead, Roberts was called to the Internal Revenue Service office—which everyone knows is a whole lot worse. The preacher is in hot water, with the IRS and other federal agencies looking into his claims and the destination of the donations he received over the years.

Spreading the Word . . . Thick

C. THOMAS PATTEN—the C he claimed stood for "cash"—and BEBE HARRISON PATTEN would have owned the world had they had access to the televangelistic pulpit of today. Patten was a hell-raising Tennessee bootlegger who got tossed out of high school for running a still in the school's basement, and his wife was a traveling fundamentalist minister. She brought him into the church and he brought her to Oakland, California, where in 1944 they set up shop in the shabby Elm Tabernacle.

Although their church was in a rundown section of Oakland, they drew a good crowd, which doubled as they advertised. She looked gorgeous in her flowing white robes, and he had a gift for collections. Between the two of them, they took in a good amount.

Patten felt proud of his method of bringing new lambs to the fold—he spent more money on advertising than anyone had ever thought possible—sometimes as much as $6,000 per week. But, the money spent in advertising proved effective, and the Pattens dragged in crowds till the small tabernacle's door nearly burst.

Moving uptown to the Oakland Women's

City Club auditorium, they accumulated such a following that they had to turn people away. The Pattens finally moved to the Oakland Arena, where eight thousand people could sit during one service; but the Arena felt too cold, so they returned to the City Club permanently. While Bebe offered her parishioners a highly personalized version of Pentecostal, her husband cajoled money from them through antics that delighted them. He begged, he pleaded, he howled, he joked.

According to writer Bernard Taper, Patten would stand before a full congregation, his head bowed in silent prayer. Then, with a wicked grin, he'd suddenly shout: "All right now, brothers and sisters, God says there's five thousand two hundred and forty dollars and fifty-five cents [or some other specific sum] that is here today that is to be taken up for His work, and God's word never fails. If God told me that money is here, it is *here*. That's a fact. How many say Amen? Hallelujah to His glorious name . . . there's three people here among you going to open their hearts to the Lord and pledge a thousand dollars each. Isn't that glorious? Everybody say Amen!"

On and on, Patten would continue until he had the full amount, and everyone knew that they could not leave the temple until Patten had the right amount. No matter what the couple needed, they could raise it in minutes. And if Patten's pleading and cajoling and yelling didn't work fast enough, he sometimes turned to bold threats—grabbing some trembling parishioner by the shoulder and screaming that God was "going to knock him off his seat" if he didn't contribute, and quick. Shades of Oral Roberts.

The Pattens opened a religious school and falsely claimed it was accredited by the neighboring University of California. C. Thomas took advantage of the postwar situation and kept the tuition extremely high, but made sure the government paid fees under the G.I. Bill.

When Patten decided to build a tabernacle on the highest hill in sin-filled San Francisco, he collected $10,000 in less than one hour. Money poured in for the tabernacle, but the structure was never built. Most money went straight into personal use by the Pattens.

Pulling one arrogant stunt too many, Patten found himself indicted for grand theft, fraud, embezzlement, and obtaining money under false pretenses. As would be expected, he turned the trial into a circus, with Patten Religious School students appearing in school sweaters with a big *P* on them and yelling "Amen!" every time the Pattens' attorneys made a point.

The district attorney proved that of the $1.4 million the Pattens took in between 1944 and 1948, less than half went to religious uses, while the balance was spent for personal use—on nine luxury cars and a cabin cruiser; on

$5,000 monthly love offerings as "allowance"; as well as to cover huge Las Vegas gambling debts.

During the trial, Patten suffered a major heart attack, but the trial continued. The jury found him guilty of five counts of grand theft, and the huckster was sentenced to between five and fifty years in state prison. Although he insisted they'd never get him behind bars, he spent three years in prison.

Allowed out on parole, he was permitted to return to his wife's pathetic Pentecostal church only on the condition that he never take up the collection. He died six years later, in 1959.

Psychic Cleric?

THE REVEREND JOHN IRISH, purportedly a Roman Catholic priest, could almost be accused of clairvoyance, since he shows up at disasters with surprising regularity. In 1987, he drew attention to himself at the Detroit Metropolitan Airport by conveniently consoling the families and friends of the victims of the Northwest Airlines crash that wiped out 156 souls.

When Detroit authorities checked on the priest's background, they found he had comforted survivors and family of at least seven other air disasters in as many states. After gaining the confidence of the victims' families, he allegedly steered them to a nice lawyer: "I have this friend who's an attorney . . ." The cleric's "friend" was Florida attorney Ronald Brimmell, who adamantly denied knowing the good father.

The Detroit Sheriff's Office, in looking into the matter, doubts that Irish is a priest—just an ambulance chaser in black suit and clerical collar. While there is no law against shepherding people to proper assistance, there is definitely a law against committing fraud.

Revirginized Love Angels

DONALD LOWERY and PAMALA ST. CHARLES—dramatically padding their own pockets and Swiss bank accounts—brought a note of happiness and hope into the lives of tens of thousands of extremely lonely men through their LOVE ANGELS of the Church of Love (COL International). As early as 1981 and advertising on postcards and by other means, COL offered potential victims a photo catalog of thirteen Love Angels to choose from as romantic pen pals and ultimate mail-order brides.

For $10, the respondent received a little magazine on the Love Angel of his choice. Throughout would be photographs of the young woman, sometimes in the nude. For a "love offering" of $15–$30, the sucker could write to a specific Love Angel, and she would write back. Each piece of correspondence cost a minimum love offering. Torrid and intimate letters ensued between the companionless men and Dawn, Terri, Vanessa, Linda, Susan, or one of the other Love Angels.

In some cases, the smitten males sent the potential girlfriend filmy underwear or negligees; the people writing the letters back to the men were encouraged to solicit such gifts, because Lowery held public sales locally and sold the delicate finery for cash. The purported Love Angel gushed over a gift in her letters, thus inviting more and better gifts.

COL's proposed goal was to create a valley paradise, Chonda-Za, where men and their Love Angels could live in wedded harmony and bliss. For a price, a man could reserve the bride he would join upon the completion of Chonda-Za. Of course, COL assured the men, donations toward Chonda-Za's construction fund would be appreciated and would definitely hasten the utopian project's finish.

Each Love Angel, COL promised the suckers, had at one time been a fallen women, a lovely wayward youngster now being "revirginized" by Mother Maria Esther Mireles (Mother Maria)—who was actually Lowery's wife. The gullible men were told that the Love Brides, in the process of being purified, were presently under protection from their harsh pasts and the outside world in a nunnerylike rustic haven near Hillsdale, Illinois. For a price, whichever bride a man chose would be as good as new by the time Chonda-Za opened for them to move in together. In the meantime, she was protected in the retreat.

After its first year in business in 1981, the Church of Love grossed over $1 million annually from lonely victims who had no idea that neither the Love Angels nor the Chonda-Za project really existed. Lowery and St. Charles's Love Bride catalog consisted of photographs of professional models—most of whom they had never even met. The two hired people—some of them men—to write the love-letter responses under the girls' names. Over the nine-year period, Lowery and St. Charles—and the letter-writers—bilked thirty-one thousand love-lorn of their savings.

For an additional $300, the men could attend a seminar where they actually got to see—but not meet in person—the Love Angels. The scantily clad purported Love Angels pranced around on the stage of a rented hall and sang hymns to their promised husbands. None of the men ever got a chance to speak with his Love Bride in person, because the young women onstage were merely actresses hired to perform. But that did not seem to bother most of the men—seeing their lovely Love Bride in the flesh was enough to keep them going.

When a dupe finally "bought" a bride, he

received a Mystic Marriage Certificate certifying that he and his Love Bride were officially "united in mystic matrimony." The certificate would be their entree into Chonda-Za when the community was finally completed.

In one case, Robert McDonald—a fifty-six-year-old, $9-an-hour Milwaukee janitor—sent nearly half his $20,000 life savings to help the Chonda-Za building fund on the promise of a servant girl of his own and a position as the utopia's head maintenance man. Besides sending COL most of his money, McDonald also named the organization as beneficiary in his will.

Only after too many flimflammed males showed up in Moline, Illinois, pestering the local police while looking for the nonexistent COL retreat in nearby Hillsdale, did the government take official action. Finally, not only the police, but the IRS, the FBI, and the U.S. Postal Investigators got in on the act. Both Lowery and St. Charles came under federal indictment; but, by turning state's evidence, Mother Maria escaped indictment.

So clever was the swindle that, to this day, many of the victims still refuse to believe they have been bamboozled—even after Lowery and St. Charles's federal convictions in February 1989 of mail fraud, conspiracy, and money laundering. Indeed, many of the hoodwinked males came to the COL's defense by contributing to what eventually added up to a $500,000 legal fund. And further, when Lowery and St.

Charles jumped bail and fled the state, their pigeons remained steadfast.

One gullible lonely heart, eighty-four-year-old Carl Cornell, appeared on Geraldo Rivera's afternoon TV talkshow to defend both his Love Bride, [the nonexistent] Dawn Mayfield, and the beleaguered Pamala St. Charles. Even when faced with the truth—that a man, and not Cornell's bride-to-be, may have written the love letters—Cornell defensively refused to admit he had been defrauded. In fact, when Rivera apologized for possibly having injured the man's feelings, Cornell said, "You're not hurting my feelings. You're hurting my friends." To save him further emotional anguish, Rivera had the man led offstage before showing the audience a taped interview in which Lowery and St. Charles described how their sting worked.

While some of the pigeons, whose feelings about COL have remained as sure as Cornell's, still look forward to Chonda-Za, it should be a long wait, what with Donald Lowery and Pamala St. Charles presently serving a combined 190 years in federal prison.

A Gila Monster in Salamander's Garb

MARK HOFMANN, well-known young dealer in religious documents, forged papers pertaining to Joseph Smith, Jr., founder of the

Church of the Latter-Day Saints. Hofmann's mid-1980s forgeries proved so believable that top members of the church accepted them, paying up to $40,000 each for nearly forty-eight of the bogus papers. Each new "discovery" brought the then-thirty-year-old collector closer to that pot of gold at the end of his Mormon rainbow.

Had Hofmann not become greedy and vengeful when his scam stalled, he might never have been caught, since his artistry had the Mormons completely fooled. But he produced a forgery that nearly destroyed the entire religion when he went too far by creating "the white salamander" paper. This paper, purportedly a letter written by Martin Harris in 1830, asserted that LDS founder Joseph Smith's angel, whose words gave Smith direction to start up the church, was in reality a white salamander—which everyone knew was an instrument of the Devil. The fake document nearly ripped the heart out of the Church, and its foundations creaked loudly.

Still not satisfied, Hofmann created a packet of papers allegedly owned by early LDS apostle Dr. William McLellin. These pages, supposedly containing many embarrassing stories about Joseph Smith, went on the auction block as the church offered $185,000 for the papers and a private investor paid $150,000 under the table.

This last bit of chicanery led to Hofmann's

downfall as well as the death of two people. In an attempt to cover up suspicion of forgery, Hofmann pipe-bombed three people on October 15, 1985 and blasted himself right out of business. Indicted for murder and theft, Hofmann saved his own life through a plea bargain. He pleaded guilty to second-degree murder and to two counts of theft by forgery or sale of nonexistent papers, which brought him a life sentence without parole, but kept him off Death Row.

In another stipulation of his plea bargain, Mark Hofmann agreed to provide complete explanations on each forgery. His "discoveries" had created an ecumenical furor that only time will heal.

The Devil Made Me Do It!

DERRY MAINWARING KNIGHT fleeced a Newick, UK, vicar and his flock of over $400,000 in a devilish scam. Vicar John Baker, fifty, hellbent on saving Knight's forty-three-year-old soul from Satanism, raised money from his parishioners—and even from friends in such high places as Parliament and nobility—to wrest Knight from the Devil's grasp.

Knight first appeared at one of the Vicar Baker's Bible study and prayer meetings. He attended frequently; and one night, after the assembly, Knight confided in the vicar an extreme problem—he was desperately in debt and needed assistance. Vicar Baker acted immediately, gathering up over $5,000 from parishioners to bail Knight out of debt. The good Anglican not only handed over the cash to Knight, but also put the stranger up in the rectory attic.

In appreciation, Knight confided something he claimed never to have shared with another soul—his deep, dark secret—that at age eight he had been told by his grandmother that he was possessed of the Devil. The old woman, a devout Satanist and dark witch, informed her impressionable young grandson that he had been born to spearhead a mighty demonic movement.

From that time on, Knight claimed to have fought the Devil within him. He had seen apparitions; he had even met Lucifer, who had confirmed that Knight was here for destruction. He had wrestled with evil and had somehow kept himself from going under. Vicar Baker, completely hornswoggled, hung on Knight's every word.

But now, the dramatic confidence man announced, he feared he might lose the fight unless he received some serious help. To rid himself of this dark curse, he would have to do financial battle with the Devil. He must undo all the evil he had created by starting up a Satanic movement, and he must do it from within. Possessed and ranting, Knight began speaking in tongues, then grabbed a Bible and ripped it to pieces. The clever con man had sought succor from the right person—Vicar Baker grabbed the Satanic ball and ran with it. He would do anything to rid the world of Knight's Satanic cult.

Within hours, Vicar Baker solicited funds from powerful people, explaining that a Christian battle against the Prince of Darkness needed enormous funding. Knight told Vicar Baker that the only way to conquer this evil was for him to buy up all the sinful gold and silver jewelry used in Satanic rituals, confiscate and destroy all the lavish robes and raiments to break the back of the vile organization. If Vicar Baker provided the funds, Knight would "sacrifice" himself by spending them against evil.

With over $150,000 in funding from Susan Sainsbury, born-again Christian wife of a supermarket millionaire and Tory member of Parliament, Vicar Baker went next to the former county high sheriff, who kicked in over $75,000. Lord Hampden, Anthony David Brand, is said to have provided Knight with a $56,000 white Rolls-Royce, complete with $4,500 scrambler phone, for his exclusive use to impress the Satanic cult members and lull them into a false sense of security. These good Christians would wrest Knight from the Devil's grip or know the reason why. They heaped money on Knight and prayed over the poor wretch's soul in a heroic effort to damn the Devil and save the man.

The police ultimately wrested Knight from his luxurious spending spree, putting him securely out of Satan's reach for a solid seven years. At his trial, the bedeviled flimflam man pointed out that he had tried to curtail Vicar Baker's enthusiasm, but things just got out of hand and no one would listen to him.

Vicar Baker insisted that had they accumulated enough money, they could have prevailed—and he was willing to continue any time Knight gave the word.

The confidence man's own mother, who had been cheated of $92,000 by her son, had the last word on the subject: "He often told me you can always take Christians for a ride because they won't take you to the law. Jail's the best thing that could happen to him!"

CHAPTER 4

Impossible Impostures

High-Flying Flimflammer

ROBERT J. HUNT—U.S. Marine fighter-pilot captain, NASA astronaut, and son of a Marine Corps colonel—spoke loftily of his adventures in weightlessness on his flight in the space shuttle *Atlantis*, of his exhilaration upon completing a bombing run on Muammar Qaddafi's illicit plant in Libya, of roaring from the deck of the aircraft carrier *Coral Sea* in his F–18 fighter plane—ready for battle.

As he mesmerized members of the Experimental Aircraft Association of Boston with his two-hour presentation in 1989, Hunt failed to mention that he also often passed himself off as a Cambridge police detective, because he lived as a confidence man with fake ID and badge and a fantastic gift for blarney that never left him at a loss for words or identities. Not only was he a bogus astronaut, but the flimflammer held no pilot's license, nor even a driver's license. Never a marine, an astronaut, or a cop, Hunt was also never the professional baseball player or real estate developer he'd led some of his friends to believe he was.

When finally carted off to prison to do twenty years for larceny and credit-card fraud, Hunt had just bilked his fourth wife, a bride of only six months, of nearly $25,000. To ensure himself a luxurious lifestyle, Hunt had surreptitiously used his new wife's business credit cards, running up huge bills. Authorities also feel convinced that Hunt still had his third wife's credit cards.

Hunt's twenty-three-year-old bride, Ann, knew nothing of her husband's three previous wives and nor his true background; the smitten young woman accepted at face value everything her doting bridegroom told her. Not until after the Massachusetts state troopers and the Cambridge police arrested Hunt did Ann find out that her dashing ex-Marine bridegroom's life had been one gigantic fabrication, and that the man she met and married in three weeks was nothing more than a charming hoodwinker.

As Ann explained after her husband's arrest and confrontation, "It was almost like watching somebody die. Here was this person I thought I knew, and bit by bit, in the course of an hour, he just dissolved, just disappeared." The bewildered young woman shook her head and choked back a tear. "I loved the person I thought he was, but that person never really existed."

On top of squeezing nearly $50,000 from his bride's family and friends in just a short few months, the flamboyant confidence man and his silver tongue convinced Dublin's Lord Mayor Briscoe that then-Prime Minister Margaret Thatcher had given Hunt—as a renowned astronaut and aviator—permission to be married in Westminster Abbey. Briscoe, not to be outdone, presented Hunt with honorary Dublin citizenship.

After honeymooning in Great Britain, the couple settled in a Medford, Massachusetts, condo. The groom, ostensibly an Annapolis graduate and top of his class, claimed to work as a Cambridge police detective; while his bride, a recent University of Rochester graduate, held an important position as optical engineer with Polaroid.

All charges initially brought against Ann were dropped, as she appeared to be one of her husband's many victims. Unfortunately, while American Express sympathized with the duped young woman, they expected the $25,000 in bills Hunt had charged to be paid. No longer working at Polaroid, the embittered young divorcee struggles to repay the debt.

Acting the Part

In 1986, part-time actors TANI FREIWALD and WES BAILEY conned three of the top four afternoon television talkshow hosts into presenting them on their shows as psychological experts and sexual perverts. Posing as one bizarre character after another, the two appeared both together and alone, stinging Oprah Winfrey, Sally Jessie Raphael, and Geraldo Rivera—and ultimately creating quite a furor.

Over the years, the two performers noted that competing talkshow hosts increasingly called out for more strange people, so the actors used various disguises to become guest experts on the shows. Freiwald, then thirty-seven and from Chicago, masqueraded as Rebecca, sex surrogate to over fifty men. Bailey, a thirty-three-year-old from Omaha, posed as one of her clients—a young married man suffering from impotency; another actress came on as his wife. Knowing that the more extreme the situation, the better, both actors stretched their talkshow impostures to the very bounds of belief.

When finally exposed, Freiwald and Bailey made headlines in *People* magazine and in most papers across the country. Even after they had been found out and thoroughly chastised and rebuked, the actors returned to the various shows under further disguises. The publicity helped their careers.

Joe Bones and the Fat Squad

JOEY SKAGGS conned his way onto *Good Morning America* in 1986 as "Joe Bones." Accompanying him were his famous "Fat Squad" and satisfied customer Stephanie Martin. For a hefty fee of $300 per day, Bones explained to David Hartman, a mean-looking Fat Squad bruiser could be rented to stand guard over someone's kitchen to make sure dieters stayed out of the refrigerator. The Fat Squad rotated in eight-hour shifts, physically restraining a dieter from going off an eating regimen—if need be, standing guard outside the bedroom door all night long.

Initially, Skaggs—if that's the forty-five-year-old "professional hoaxer's" real name, and there seems to be some doubt about that—sent out press releases to the media, announcing the existence of the Fat Squad under the auspices of Joe Bones. The *Washington Post* responded, phoning for an interview. After speaking with Skaggs, who passed himself off as Joe Bones, the reporter called the list of satisfied "clients," who were actually actors prepared in advance by Skaggs.

Satisfied with Bones's veracity, the *Post* ran the story; and three days later, a reporter from the *Philadelphia Inquirer* called Bones. When a piece on the Fat Squad went out over the *Inquirer*'s national Knight-Ridder wire service, the entire country picked it up. At that point, Joe Bones received invitations to be interviewed from *Good Morning America* and Cable News Network.

Before his hoax concluded, Bones and the

Fat Squad had made appearances on British and French television. The day after Skaggs and his group of actors arrived at CBS in the limousines sent to bring them to the *Good Morning America* show, Skaggs gave out the real story of the hoax to the *New York Post*. Although the following day, David Hartman good-naturedly admitted to having been had, "in spades," he had no idea just how big a sting Skaggs had played.

Skaggs explained that under a number of aliases he had been running harmless hoaxes for over twenty-five years in an effort to educate the public. He preferred to call his hoaxes "stings," for art's sake. He considered himself a performer whose acting ability had won him validity and media coverage through his hoaxes. He hoped that, by gross exaggeration, his stings would make people more aware of the kinds of scams real con artists run.

Proud of his stings, Skaggs pointed out that this was not his first time on Hartman's show; just one year earlier, also as Joe Skaggs, he had appeared as the inventor of a fish-tank condominium for "upwardly mobile" guppies. Hartman seemed as fascinated as he was amused by the guppy condos that came equipped with completely furnished living rooms, bathrooms, and kitchens.

Besides creating a celebrity sperm bank where women could become impregnated by the likes of Bob Dylan, Paul McCartney, or

Mick Jagger, he also took on the mantle of world-famous entomologist "Dr. Josef Gregor." Skaggs based this hoax on Franz Kafka's *Metamorphosis*, in which a man named Gregor turns into a six-foot roach. For this sting, Skaggs claimed to have manufactured cockroach hormones that would cure all the ills in the world—from arthritis to menstrual cramps—and even protected people from nuclear radiation.

When the story hit the media, Skaggs expected people to be amused. Sadly, the public clamored for the roach hormone, willing to pay any amount for the preposterous protection it purportedly offered. In disgust, Skaggs called the *Wall Street Journal* to blow the whistle on this hoax himself, since so many people wanted the nonexistent roach hormone.

The man's still out there, perhaps as Bones, perhaps as Skaggs, perhaps as someone else. Just look for a man offering some strange concoction or hard-to-believe idea—that'll be Joe Bones.

Six Degrees of Invasion

DAVID HAMPTON invaded Manhattan with all the panache of a confidence man three times his age, but youth was on his side. The eldest son of a Buffalo, New York, attorney, the then seventeen-year-old Hampton had been a precocious child and an impossible teen, fancying himself much too glamorous and talented to languish in such a dismal locale as Buffalo and deeming Paris or Rome more his style. He spoke three languages, dreamed of becoming an actor, and knew his light-skinned black good-looks and glib tongue would help him no matter what his endeavor. Thus his life's direction seemed almost inevitable.

Shuttled from one expensive prep school to another, the "misunderstood" young Hampton finally caused one problem too many for his father, who refused to provide any further support to a son who disdained such normal goals as law school, medical school, or business college.

In 1981, young Hampton headed for Manhattan and a possible theatrical career. While out clubbing one night, he and another teen friend failed abysmally on their first attempt to gain entrance to the fabulous Studio 54—the doorman arbitrarily refused them admission. Unlike most people who, when turned away from such an elegant club for no apparent reason, would walk away and try another club, Hampton took the rebuff personally and resolved to force the Studio 54 guards to lift the ban.

With all the ingenuity of a fantasy-based teenager, Hampton and his friend orchestrated a surefire scheme of imposture that blasted open the doors at Studio 54 and elsewhere. Posing as the only son of Academy Award–winning superstar-director Sidney Poitier—who lived in Hollywood and had only daughters, but who knew?—Hampton, accompanied by his friend, purposely pulled up to the club's curb in a rented stretch limousine.

The friend jumped out first and dramatically asked people to make way for Poitier's son. The guards at the door, obviously blinded by the trappings and never for a moment recognizing the two teenagers they had rebuffed just a short time before, ushered the two teenagers in with great fanfare and no check of IDs. The magical name of Poitier parted the crowds, and, once inside, all drinks were on the house. Hampton discovered that play-acting Poitier's nonexistent son might very well bring him everything but the key to the city.

A year later, "David Poitier" showed up at the doorstep of an actor-director who was house-sitting screen star Melanie Griffith's Manhattan apartment. Hampton explained that "close-friend Melanie" usually opened her place to him when he was in town. Never doubting the young man's word, the convinced house-sitter allowed Hampton to sleep on the sofa.

Having deduced the mileage he could gain from his Poitier imposture, Hampton wandered on to the Connecticut College campus and bunked with students there, becoming a professional guest. Upon leaving the campus, he pilfered an address book from one of the students with which he gained entrance to exclusive Manhattan homes. Calling private home phone numbers from the little book and mentioning the right college students' names opened some extremely exclusive—and trusting—doors in the blink of an eye and without question.

When the imposturing teenager called Lea and John Jay Iselin—then president of WNET, New York City's public television station—introduced himself as Poitier's son and good friend of their daughter Josie and told them he was out from Hollywood and had just been mugged on his way in from the airport, the Iselins took him into their home for the night and lent him $20.

The next day, savoring his success, Hampton tried the same scam on Osborn Elliott, then dean of Columbia University's Graduate School of Journalism. Growing ever bolder, in the middle of the night Hampton brought in a young gentleman friend. The next day, a shocked and flustered Inger Elliott found Hampton and another youth asleep in the guest bed together. Hampton passed the young friend off as Malcolm Forbes's nephew.

Charismatic and genteel, Hampton bounced from one luxurious New York City apartment to another before someone thought to check to see if Sidney Poitier did indeed have a son. When it was discovered that young Hampton was a fraud, the people he had freeloaded pressed felonious charges, sizzling with anger at Hampton's charade. The teen—on a plea-bargain, pleading guilty to a reduced charge of attempted burglary—received a suspended sentence with a proviso that he leave New York City and never return.

The flamboyant Hampton, however, envisioning himself as a celebrity guest who provided New Yorkers a service by livening up their parties, could not stay away from Manhattan. When he checked into a NYC hotel as David Poitier, he found himself arrested again and imprisoned for nearly two years.

Most people might have learned a lesson from a two-year stint behind bars and would have steered clear of a city where the authorities emphasized their displeasure by handing out prison sentences, but possibly young Hampton had a warped learning curve. After three years allegedly in Paris, Rome, and London, where he claimed to have alternately worked, sponged off others, and thrived as a gigolo, Hampton rushed back to New York City, eager to start up where he left off before his last conviction.

In a metropolis of such a vast number of faceless people, Hampton—who had worn out his welcome on the society party circuit in the Big Apple—could easily have lived the rest of his life in New York City without ever having been discovered by the authorities. But for the publicity-seeking twenty-two-year-old, anonymity would prove stifling, and Hampton ran true to form.

Alighting from a taxicab, Hampton refused to pay the fare, thus calling attention to himself. The cabbie summoned the police and had the flamboyant young man arrested. When Hampton failed to show up in court on the misdemeanor charges brought by the cabbie, he insisted he had been unable to make the court date because of a traffic injury for which he was hospitalized.

When Hampton finally made an appearance in municipal court, he provided the judge with written proof of his ambulance trip. Fined $500 for not paying his cab fare, and given another suspended sentence, Hampton might have gotten away with his ambulance fabrication; but someone noticed the paperwork he presented had been falsified. The authorities immediately arrested the young scam artist again, this time for forging official papers.

David Hampton's antics might have gone virtually unnoticed by most of the world, except that playwright John Guare became so fascinated with the young flimflammer that he wrote a play about Hampton's various escapades. *Six Degrees of Separation*, closely following the teenager's impostures, became a critically acclaimed Tony-nominated comedy-drama that played to packed houses at New York City's Lincoln Center.

Hampton created further headlines when he insisted he should receive a piece of the play's profits, because without him, there would be no play. He went so far as to seek a court injunction to keep the play from continuing until someone gave him his due share.

Reveling in the publicity surrounding his impostures, Hampton appears on whichever television and radio talkshows will have him. Although Hampton officially announced to the media he wants a career in acting, when the play first opened in a small theater, he said he would rather "be known for positive achievements than as a slickster in an Off-Broadway play."

To Princeton Via Prison

JAMES ARTHUR HOGUE came from Kansas City, Kansas, where he lettered on the high school cross-country team and still holds his school's records for one- and two-mile runs. After a short time at the University of Wyoming, where he ran in only one accredited meet, he transferred to the University of Texas for a couple of years before dropping out of school completely in 1983.

With the face and body of a young boy, the

twenty-five-year-old long-distance runner popped up at Palo Alto High School in northern California as Jay Huntsman. He claimed to be a teenager whose parents both died in Bolivia. For the past eight years, he alleged, he had lived in a commune in Elko, Nevada, which was why he didn't have the proper papers. He ran cross-country for his new high school.

Unfortunately for the counterfeit teenager, a reporter from a local newspaper—Jason Cole of the *Peninsula Times-Tribune*—set about writing up a story on this unusual newcomer who had just run in the local cross-country meet. The deeper Cole dug into the young man's background, the less he came up with. Cole discovered there was no commune in Elko, and realized he was on to a much bigger story than "orphaned runner hits town." Cole prepared his case carefully, since it appeared explosive.

The day before Cole's exposé ran in the local newspaper, Huntsman/Hogue bolted. His story made the news wires, and the entire country learned that a twenty-five-year-old man had enrolled as an eighteen-year-old student and had kept up with runners nearly ten years his junior.

The law finally caught up with Hogue, and the flimflammer was convicted of check forgery and sentenced to probation. But the lithe runner took off for Colorado, where he conned his way into a position as instructor at a cross-country training camp in Vail by virtue of his "Ph.D. from Stanford." Unfortunately for Hogue, eventually one of the runners recognized the new instructor as the fraudulent "Huntsman" from Palo Alto High School and reported him to the camp's founder, who confronted the young man. Hogue offered no explanation or response.

Some time before being discovered and while still working in Vail, Hogue had met and befriended a vacationing California bicycle designer. One day shortly after leaving Colorado, Hogue showed up at the bicycle designer's home north of San Francisco. The young man worked in the bicycle shop for his keep for several weeks and then took off with $20,000 worth of the designer's tools and other goods from the shop.

More bad luck for Hogue—in a matter of months after leaving California, he was arrested again. A cyclist in Utah bought a precision tool from the runner and then recognized the bicycle designer's name on the tool. The cyclist phoned the designer, who called the police. Although convicted on possession of stolen property—yet not for the theft itself—Hogue received a five-year sentence but spent only ten months in prison.

The bicycle designer pleaded with the Utah courts to keep Hogue in prison and not allow him out on parole, but they ignored the victim's warnings that Hogue was more than he appeared and would disappear as soon as released from prison.

During his prison term, Hogue applied to several Ivy League universities as Alexi Indris-Santana, a nineteen-year-old, self-educated cowboy from a ranch in Utah. The thirty-one-year-old passed the Scholastic Aptitude Test with exceptionally high test scores, and his falsified letters of recommendation glowed. Before his release from Utah prison in 1988, the clever masquerader received letters of acceptance from both Brown and Princeton—along with regrets from Yale and Harvard.

Santana/Huntsman/Hogue chose Princeton but requested a postponement of enrollment so he could have time to take care of his dying mother. The university officials not only granted his request, they offered him a $40,000 scholarship. As soon as the prison officials opened the door and allowed Hogue out, he jumped parole and disappeared, just as the bicycle designer had predicted.

In February 1991, Santana/Huntsman/Hogue felt cold handcuffs snap around his wrists in front of his stunned classmates in geology class as a Princeton Borough detective shackled the young man on a felony fugitive warrant. James Hogue's brilliant athletic career ultimately did him in, because a Yale runner at an Ivy League meet, who had attended Palo Alto High School, recognized Hogue as a former classmate.

Instead of confronting the flimflammer, the Yale runner called the track coach in Palo Alto and asked him what she should do. The coach advised her to do nothing, that he would take care of the matter. He immediately called Jason Cole, the reporter who initially unmasked Hogue. Cole jumped at the chance to break an even bigger story than before. He called Princeton, telling them who they had on their hands, and then broke the story locally before it went to the wire services.

Thus, the unsuspecting con artist had to have another day in court, this time in Trenton, New Jersey. A brilliant scholar and an even more remarkable athlete, Hogue had it all. But at press time, he faces four felony counts—three on forgery and one on theft by deception. Once Hogue is released from New Jersey prison, Utah would like to have the perennial student back.

The Queen of Welfare Fraud

DOROTHY MAE WOODS had everything a young black woman from a destitute sharecropper family in the Deep South could ever want: a loving second husband whose degree in engineering and way with people placed his earning power far beyond that of most men of color; eight beautiful, healthy children, all well-dressed and receiving the finest of educations; a sprawling Spanish-style mansion in the most elegant section of wealthy Pasadena, California; three new, gaudy, luxury automobiles; and all the jewels, furs, and designer clothes she could wear. But that wasn't enough for Dorothy Mae. She needed excitement, and her numerous trips to Las Vegas just never quite satisfied her lust for thrills.

In pursuit of more and better and wilder, Dorothy Mae Woods clipped the people of Illinois for over $250,000, while at the same time taking the state of California for well over $377,000. In the process, she became nationally known as the U.S. Welfare Queen. Supermarket weeklies had a field day, local newspapers gave her headlines, and television talkshows offered her a chance to tell her side of the story. Audacious, flamboyant, and fun-loving, she garnered more than her fifteen minutes of celebrity.

At sixteen, the Hermanville, Mississippi, sharecropper's daughter married a Chicago numbers runner and alleged drug dealer. How and when she began her life of crime is not known, but the city of Chicago finally went after her for fraudulent use of stolen credit cards. While the district attorney's office suspected she and a confederate had charged well over $500,000 in merchandise, they went for prosecution on a little less than $250,000—none of which was ever recovered. After serving six months of a two-year sentence, she was paroled on the condition that she leave Illinois immediately and never come back to Chicago.

Woods gratefully returned to her Pasadena mansion, which she had filled with felonious purchases from her Chicago caper—plush furniture, fragile lamps, and luxurious linens. But when her alleged drug-dealing husband returned to Chicago, leaving her with the children and no income, her need for cash flow, and ultimately, her avarice, drove her to commit welfare fraud on a monumental scale.

"It never occurred to me to liquidate instead of perpetuate, and my need became a greed," she said in playful rhyming speech. "Besides," she pointed out with a quick grin, "there was no way I could let go of my fancy lifestyle. That would have been too embarrassing."

Dorothy Mae, faced with no lawful means of support, refused to sell anything from her mansion, situated in one of the area's most lavish neighborhoods, next door to the palatial home of Los Angeles's then-district attorney. With a Rolls-Royce, Cadillac, and Mercedes-Benz parked in the driveway, Dorothy explained, she felt she was somebody. Instead of parting with her possessions, the enterprising young woman filed for state and county welfare, claiming the servants' quarters in a small shack in the rear of the mansion as her only residence.

Because of Dorothy Mae's large number of

dependent children, the welfare check proved substantial. No one asked any questions, since the plump young black woman fit the profile of a beleaguered welfare mother—she dressed the part, wearing rags, a ratty wig, and little or no jewelry, and acted contritely ashamed of being forced to ask for public assistance.

Dorothy's expenses, however, were great, and her welfare check covering Aid to Dependent Children just was not enough—not with a well-landscaped mansion and huge cars to keep up, and a high life that called for a steady influx of funds.

In 1974, a year after her divorce from the alleged drug dealer became final, Dorothy married John Woods. A real estate executive, Woods had a college degree in engineering and was as far removed in background and education from her previous husband as two people could be. Although John knew of his wife's fraudulent activities, he said nothing and allowed her to continue fleecing the government. He claims he never participated in the actual fraud, but he nevertheless actively shared in the cashing and spending of the ill-gotten gains. Trips to Las Vegas to gamble away the county's money became a regular weekend pastime. Spending sprees were routine.

Needing more money, Dorothy Mae reasoned that most welfare workers were white or Hispanic and saw so many black women, they would not be able to tell one from the other. She donned another wig and posed as Dorothy Palmer, claiming her residence to be in one of the low-income Los Angeles slum apartment buildings she owned. To ensure not being caught, Dorothy Mae went to a different county office to file the new claim—and obtained another welfare check with all the benefits of food stamps and free state medical care for herself and her children.

Dorothy Mae, who now owned several ghetto rentals, found the ruse so easily accomplished that she changed names and identities to obtain even more welfare checks. Before she married John, she was already balancing six new identities—quite a dowry.

After her marriage to Woods, Dorothy Mae added six more aliases and a total of forty-nine children. She made blank birth and baptism certificates for herself and her fake kids by Xeroxing the originals and erasing the names and dates. She then typed in new data as the need presented itself. She had driver's licenses, Social Security cards, and other identification under all twelve aliases.

Dorothy Mae's taste for the good life increased with each new welfare identity, and she spent most of the money as fast as it came in, investing some by accumulating low-income "rentals." The rest went for luxury appliances, furs, designer clothes, fine jewelry, bars of silver, and still more expensive cars.

When a county welfare worker made an appointment with her to visit her at one of her slum apartments under one of her assumed names, she would "borrow" neighborhood children to augment her own. Each impersonation called for a different slum residence, a change of wig, and a whole new identity. At one location, she had red hair and posed as Claretha Adams; at another, she was Genaview Bowen, a brunette—twelve wigs, twelve identities. And with each wig, she took on a different personality, stretching her acting ability to its fullest. Quick with a smile and a hearty laugh, a steady gaze, and cheerful demeanor, none of her dozen personae was ever questioned by her twelve caseworkers.

In playing the role of a long-suffering single mother stuck with so many young children, Dorothy Mae used such inventive aliases as Sarah Burks, Esther Evans, Arlene Grant, Florence Jackson, Bernice Mays, Roxie Marborough, Dorothy Prince, Patricia Waytes, and Victoria Youngblood. Her forty-nine fictitious children among the real were Anna Merle, Betty, Freddy, Jason, Johnny, Leonard, Leonidas, Leora, Leroy, Leslie, Lisa, Mary, Roxanne, Ruth, and Willie.

John and Dorothy Mae Woods enjoyed life to the hilt for nearly nine years, producing five more children of their own. But one day early in 1980, a friend visiting the Pasadena mansion spotted some welfare checks on the desk with the rest of the mail and tried to blackmail the couple. When the Woods refused to pay her, the woman promptly turned them in to the authorities.

When the law arrived with a search warrant, Dorothy Mae and her children had mysteriously vanished, leaving husband John to mind the house and hold whatever bag might be presented.

The moment Dorothy Mae had suspected the game might be up, she packed her eight minor children off to a $12,000-a-month apartment in Kingston, Jamaica, enrolling them all in an elegant private school. They lived in splendor for almost a year while the thoroughly baffled authorities tried to track them down.

The Woods's mind-boggling paper trail proved complicated indeed, and the accumulation of enough evidence for a grand jury indictment took well over a year. Once the government officials felt sufficiently prepared, they faced the problem of finding Dorothy Mae, who had done a marvelous job of eluding them. Another anonymous tip, however, informed the law of Dorothy Mae's plush Caribbean whereabouts.

While the authorities asserted Dorothy Mae had illegally fled the country to avoid prosecution, she insisted from exile that no one had tried to arrest her. She claimed she just wanted to protect her children from the harassment of invasive media. When she and her children left Southern California, there had been no indictment, only public speculation of wrong-doing.

When she refused to return to California voluntarily—and she had not committed an extraditable crime—the Jamaican authorities worked behind the scenes with the U.S. government and forcibly put Dorothy Mae and her children on a plane bound for Miami. The FBI greeted her at the Miami airport with a federal warrant and placed her in the Dade County jail under $250,000 bail while awaiting extradition to California.

During her nine-year imposture, from 1971 to 1980, Dorothy Mae Woods received a maximum of $5,162 each month in welfare checks, resulting in an overall $377,458 in cash and an additional undetermined amount in food stamps and free state medical aid. When her assets were finally seized, the authorities found $14,000 worth of uncashed welfare checks and $100,000 in food-stamp and medical benefits.

At the time of their arrest, the Woods were estimated to be worth $2.5 million. The entire fortune was confiscated, and Dorothy Mae spent eight years in prison. When the judge passed sentence on her, he commented on her boundless greed, saying, "I'm sorry I can only give you eight years." Her husband received a lesser sentence and custody of the children for having cooperated with the courts.

Authorities insist that they know of no one in this country's history who ever took the

U.S. welfare system for more than did Dorothy Mae Woods. In a final footnote, Dorothy Mae served her full eight-year prison term, earning an AA degree in Human Behavior from the University of La Verne while still behind bars. She plans to receive her B.A. in Sociology from the California State University at Los Angeles this year.

Dorothy Mae Woods insists she is completely rehabilitated; but one of her former attorneys has serious reservations, mentioning something about a leopard's spots.

The Grand Impostor

STANLEY CLIFFORD WEYMAN—aka Royal St. Cyr, S. Clifford Weinberg, Ethan Allen Weinberg, Rodney S. Wyman, Sterling C. Wyman, and C. Sterling Weinberg—changed personae almost as easily as he did his socks. A drab clerk from Brooklyn, he made many trips to prison for his impostures before he finally discovered how to avoid arrest—as a U.S. consul delegate to Morocco, then as a military attaché from Serbia, a Rumanian consul general, and a commander in the Rumanian army.

His early-twentieth-century impostures boldly demonstrated the man's ability to maneuver people. First as Commander, and then Captain

Rodney Sterling Wyman, he led the White House on a merry chase when he posed as the State Department Naval Liaison Officer—a position that did not exist until he created it. In his fictitious capacity, Weyman hoodwinked his way into arranging a meeting between an Afghan princess and President Harding after the White House had refused to see her.

Always ready to fill a vacuum, and never at a loss for creativity, Weyman heard that high-echelon White House officials found Afghanistan's Princess Fatima politically undesirable and refused to extend her a formal invitation to meet the President. The hoaxer, in full pseudonaval uniform, passed himself off to the princess as a White House liaison officer and insinuated that he had entree to the President. Although there would be "expenses" involved, he might be persuaded to set up a meeting for the princess with President Harding.

The princess, wealthy almost beyond measure, showed her generosity and finally turned over $10,000 to purchase "gifts for high officials." The swindler pretended to be an undersecretary in the State Department, bamboozled his way into the White House, and escorted the princess into the Oval Office. Through all his machinations, he later befriended Woodrow Wilson.

The confidence man's acting ability proved so great that Viennese Dr. Adolf Lorenz, noted for his bloodless surgery, even took "Dr. Weyman" on as an assistant. This sham came to an end when the imposter's lack of medical skills became too apparent.

Dr. Weyman reached what some would consider the height of his audacity when he posed as a prison reform expert, speaking first at Sing Sing Prison, where he delivered a harangue against capital punishment, and later lectured at Middlesex University on the topic, "Insanity: its defense in crime." This talk he turned into an attack against prison psychiatrists, suggesting that they be "subjected to a searching mental examination."

CHAPTER 5

Fanciful Flimflammers

The Hurly-Burly Man

J. BAM MORRISON perpetrated the classic "circus advanceman" con throughout the United States but never suspected the bizarre twist his game would take. For a number of years, the audacious huckster crisscrossed the Midwest, conning townspeople out of their hard-earned cash and anything else he could squeeze from them. When the tall, gregarious James Garner-type scam artist stumbled onto the sleepy but prosperous little town of Wetumka, Oklahoma, on a hot day in July 1950, he must have thought he had died and gone to heaven.

As he sized up the pleasant, trusting faces of the friendly townsfolk after having chatted with several, the professional flimflam man in him knew the little burg was definitely virgin territory—no one had ever run a scam on these congenial Wetumkans, and they were more than ripe for the plucking.

Morrison boldly strode into the local newspaper office and announced that the circus was coming! Bohn's United Circus, the traveling bigtop Morrison claimed to work for as advance publicity man, had chosen Wetumka as its next site. The biggest spectacle this side of the Mississippi, he exclaimed, would be arriving in Wetumka in less than three weeks, on July 24.

The excited news publisher dragged Morrison to the Wetumka town council, and the local officials immediately set up a special emergency meeting of the chamber of commerce. The affable hustler with his permanent grin warned everyone that they had better stock up on supplies, because the cozy little town of less than three thousand people was about to be inundated by thousands of folks from miles around coming to see the traveling circus.

"Yes, sir," Morrison crooned, his florid cheeks glistening, "this is gonna be the biggest thing to ever hit Wetumka! Crowds'll pour into this beautiful little hamlet from a dozen towns around—mebbe more. Yes sir, folks, you'd better lay in those supplies, cuz you're definitely gonna need 'em."

And, he added, anybody buying advertising space on the circus grounds—either on a billboard or on the side of the canvas tent—would be eligible to sell the circus his products or services. The likable con man explained that the circus would be willing to purchase all its supplies from Wetumka's merchants—hotdogs and other refreshments, even hay for the horses and elephants—if they bought advertising space. Whipping the chamber of commerce into a near-frenzy of greed, Morrison assured the naive town fathers that everyone in the community stood to make a gigantic profit from the project.

Excitement spread as the con artist sold advertising space on the side of the circus tent and on billboards and in a circus flier, and advertising time on the circus's truck loudspeaker. The gullible Wetumka merchants swallowed his promises and bought heavily, treating Morrison royally as he sold them his bill of goods. While he pretended to be making elaborate preparations for his nonexistent circus, handing out free passes to almost everyone, he settled in as a guest of the town.

Free of charge, Morrison roomed at the local hotel, took all his meals at the best restaurant in town, had his hair cut and nails done at the local barber, and his clothes cleaned by the local cleaners. In exchange for free passes, the local physician treated him for minor complaints at no charge.

The flimflammer warned the manager of the tiny Meadors Hotel that the circus loudspeaker truck usually travels at least fifty miles out in ever-widening circles around the circus site, attracting many thousands of visitors; so the hotelier should prepare for an onslaught of out-of-towners who would need a place to stay overnight. The elated manager took Morrison at his word and purchased all new mattresses for the overflow. The forewarned butcher stocked up on hotdogs; the baker, on ingredients for buns. The feed shop owner ordered tons of hay for the elephants and other circus livestock.

In exchange for a whopping chunk of advertising space, restaurant owner Louis Charlton received a huge contract to feed all the circus personnel. Out of gratitude, he provided the slick trickster with his very best fare at no charge. The convivial con artist, now a friendly fixture in town, greeted everyone he met on the street with a wide grin and free circus passes. The local Boy Scout troup volunteered for hurly-burly duty and, with the insistence of Morrison, even became the official sponsors of the circus. The town prepared while Morrison sold ads and wallowed hip-deep in luxury.

Although Morrison felt as if he'd found paradise and really didn't want it to end, he knew it must, as his carpetbag fairly bulged to overflowing with the townspeople's money.

A week before the circus was supposed to arrive, when Morrison had sold advertising space or time to every Wetumkan who would buy, he announced to the mayor and town council that he had to get back to the circus to make final preparations for the publicity. With his usual enthusiasm, the jovial flimflam man pumped up the town council, painting a picture for them, telling them to listen for the circus one week hence:

"At noon on July twenty-fourth, off in the distance, you're gonna hear the calliope and the circus band and the trumpeting of the elephants and the roar of lions and tigers. Then you're gonna see the dust of the parade as the circus heads into town. First to arrive'll be the circus clowns—they always lead the procession, those madcap merrymakers. The tumblers and jugglers'll follow, and then acrobats and the cages of wild animals. Everybody in makeup and costumes. Oh, what a day that'll be!"

When Morrison—his pockets nearly ripped open with last-minute cash—left the citizens of Wetumka, they were in a frenzy of excited anticipation.

In the meantime, the overeager newspaper publisher, unable to wait for the circus's official advertising, printed full-page ads in his paper each day announcing the circus's pending arrival in Wetumka. He also made up thousands of handbills, which the Boy Scouts were only too happy to distribute far and wide. In fact, the news publisher did such a good job of advertising that no one in town seemed to notice that the circus's ads never materialized.

Besides, everyone was too busy with preparations.

On July 24, throngs from everywhere showed up in Wetumka to see the circus. The hotel filled to overflowing, the restaurants and coffee shops had long lines, and merchants knew they would sell out everything they had stocked for the occasion. The massive crowds of people from all over waited for the circus with growing enthusiasm.

By noon, people several rows deep lined the main street of town waiting for the big parade. Wetumka had never seen so many people. Folks stared down the street, first one way, then the other. They grew impatient, then unruly. When it became apparent that there would be no circus, the crowd turned surly, holding the distraught mayor and town council directly responsible for their disappointment. People couldn't decide whether to sue or tear down the town.

Before the people got out of hand, just half an hour after the circus parade should have arrived, the mayor received a postage-due package containing a handful of hay and a card reading, "Regards, J. Bam Morrison." It was all just one big scam! And storeowners whose orders dealt directly with the circus found themselves stuck with everything they had ordered. Realizing the townsfolk had been humbugged and were themselves guilty of false advertising—and to save their hides and placate the people who had come from miles around just to see a circus—the mayor admitted they had been hornswaggled and announced the advent of the first annual Sucker Day.

And the town council declared that all concessionaires should give away free of charge all the hotdogs, soda pop, and other refreshments, along with all the balloons, banners, and other circus souvenirs.

This pleased the crowd so much that they in turn did a land-office business in town, spending all the cash they had brought to go through at the circus. The ecstatic town merchants watched what could have been a fiscal tragedy turn into a fantastic financial success.

So thrilled with the unexpected results of Morrison's fleecing, Wetumka residents celebrate July 24 every year as Sucker Day with a parade and street fair. Since 1950, Sucker Day stands as the biggest event on Wetumka's social calendar.

When a sheriff from a town in Missouri called Wetumka to ask if the law there was interested in extraditing Morrison when he'd served out his sentence in Missouri, the Oklahomans told the sheriff there was no warrant out after him and no charges to be brought; but they would be happy to have him as their guest of honor for the next Sucker Day—if he paid his own way there.

Uncle Sam's Bad Boy

"Financier" MICHAEL RAPP took New York's Flushing Federal Savings & Loan for well over $8 million in 1984 by putting up worthless securities as collateral for loans. The FSLIC had to make good, which ultimately came out of the taxpayers' pocket.

In Orlando, Rapp swooped down on the Florida Center Bank and clipped it for $30 million. From California to New York to Florida, Rapp fleeced one financial institution after another with near-impunity as the law looked the other way and Rapp made off with millions.

Why? Because back in the 1970s, the man known as Michael Rapp had really been Michael Hellerman, a mildly notorious bunco artist whose kiss-and-tell biography, *Wall Street Swindler*, named some pretty hefty names in the underworld. By assisting the federal government to put away nearly three dozen mobsters, crooked politicians, and dishonest stockbrokers, Hellerman fell under the federal witness program. In return for his assistance in collaring so many big-time crooks, the government gave Hellerman a fortuitous change of name and trade rather than a deserved change of address to the nearest federal penitentiary.

Set up with a new identity as Michael Rapp and a new occupation as a restaurant operator on Cape Cod, federally protected Hellerman/Rapp had quite literally been given a license to steal—by the federal government. Unfortunately for Uncle Sam, this nephew's vast appetite for the good life and gaming capitals of the world could not be sated on a restaurateur's wages; so, as Rapp, with no hint of embezzler Hellerman in his newly—and officially—created background, the confessed swindler was able to rip off eager victims who checked Rapp's spotless past thoroughly before investing with him. Anyone checking up on the man would have access only to the federal government's carefully whitewashed history, with no hint of his true criminal background to forewarn them.

Bartholomew Lee, a San Francisco attorney representing one of the firms hoodwinked by Hellerman/Rapp, is quoted as saying, "The U.S. created a person who could, in fact if not intention, cause significant damage to a federally insured institution. Now Uncle Sam has to foot the bill for what its errant child has done."

Upon pursuing the matter, the media came up with the two identities for the same man. With all this new notoriety, Hellerman/Rapp may never get his day in court to defend himself against his latest victims. The many bitter heavyweights he testified against and sent off to federal penitentiary will more than likely arrange to save the federal government the time and the money for a trial or a new identity.

While Hellerman/Rapp's colorful exploits may be fascinating, the convicted stock swindler's shortsightedness is not so admirable and may well prove fatal.

Pitching the Bull with Bluebloods

CLYDE B. PITCHFORD, JR., took the abundantly wealthy residents of Richmond, Virginia, for nearly $700,000 through felonious machinations at E.F. Hutton and Dean Witter stock brokerages. A thirty-one-year-old, very promising stockbroker, Pitchford had winning ways and a confidence man's heart. His schemes went so well, and his charm proved so great that he even planned to run for governor.

Starting life inauspiciously in Norfolk, Virginia, the son of a chemical salesman and a bridal-shop proprietor, young Pitchford worked his way through school at the University of Richmond with a job in a clothing store. His face and body covered with angry acne, the shy young man tried his best to blend into the scenery and stay out of ridicule's way. Not until his facial scars calmed down after graduation did he muster up enough nerve to approach the world; then his winning ways did the rest.

In 1977, Pitchford volunteered to work on Virginia's lieutenant-gubernatorial campaign for State Senator Joe Canada and therein found his niche. A fast learner, the recent college graduate observed just how much power vast sums of money wielded as he threw himself into the fundraising and financial work for the Republican party. After taking stock of what qualities prompted respect and admiration in others, the young man from modest beginnings carefully rewrote his own personal upbringing to impress and manipulate people.

Two years later, when Pitchford went to work for stock brokers at Dean Witter, he convinced everyone there he was a true Virginia blueblood. The stories of his family background grew and blossomed, as he found people loved to rub elbows with high society. He good-naturedly complained of his mother's irresponsibility at spending $200,000 annually on her florist's bill and the amount of care needed to run the family plantations. His complaints only served to solidify his bogus background.

By 1983, Pitchford switched stockerage firms and aligned himself with E.F. Hutton, where, with his soft-spoken manner and his maturing good looks, he easily conned everyone into believing his fabricated lofty breeding. While he perfected his upper-class stance, he discovered he had an uncanny ability—with what appeared to be a Midas touch, the young power broker could turn people's portfolios into gold before siphoning off some for himself to augment his $35,000 annual salary.

Pitchford's popularity grew, as did his feigned reputation as a member of the privileged upper-class. Actual members of the elite country-club set accepted him as one of their own, and he became close friends with many of the most influential people in the state. He enjoyed a chauffeured Rolls-Royce, rode to the hounds at the Deep Run Hunt Club, relaxed at the Commonwealth Club, and even played squash with U.S. Senator John Warner.

The fraudulent blueblood, however, could not leave well enough alone, unsatisfied with everything he had attained. He wanted more—that "big deal" that always seemed to be right around the corner. He borrowed $400,000 from the Bank of Virginia by forging his partners' signature on the loan application. With this money, he further increased the supplement of his lowly income so he could live high and keep up with the correct Joneses.

But when the payments on the loan became too difficult to manage, the young swindler panicked and joined into a clandestine partnership with a clever financier he had just met—Michael Rapp. The two confidence men bought the struggling Florida Center Bank in

Orlando and planned to make it flourish or milk it dry. With their combined expertise, they felt they might be able to make a go of the project, and what better source for capital than extending themselves loans from their own bank.

Pitchford, friends said later, fully intended to make enough from the purchase of the bank to pay back all the clients' accounts he had embezzled from—before someone discovered his theft. After he had covered the past, he looked forward to a good income for himself. Unfortunately, two weeks into the Florida enterprise, bank examiners stepped in and refused to accept Pitchford's $250,000 loan application.

With his plan gone awry and nothing except his small salary coming in to handle his gargantuan debts, the young man disappeared. With the FBI on his trail, he stayed out of sight for over three months before finally giving himself up to the federal authorities. During those three months, all of Richmond seemed completely bonkers over Pitchford. Someone wrote "The Ballad of Clyde Pitchford," and the song received Top Ten status on the local radio station. People displayed posters, bumper stickers and T-shirts with "Where's Clyde?" on them.

While Pitchford sat contritely in the city jail under federal detention, Richmond residents and people from miles around crowded the Arthur Ashe Athletic Center almost to bursting when Pitchford's belongings went on the auction block. His antiques and other possessions brought in $104,000 to help pay off his creditors. New York publishers rushed to get his signature on a book contract.

Ironically, although most of the bluebloods he charmed into friendship turned their backs on him, some did not. Those who stayed staunchly behind him make excuses for his actions and praise the man highly for his better qualities, which were what they were drawn to in the first place. It remains to be seen whether they'll be there for him when he finally gets out of prison.

Fraudulent Tax Shelters

WILLIAM A. KIRKPATRICK used tax shelters as his hook to part suckers from their money, talking them into buying penny stocks that he touted as the best possible protection from having to pay taxes. But even when the IRS and the federal government's tax reform took the wind out of most investment swindlers' sales, the Denver promoter held in there, bilking investors of almost $300 million. Kirkpatrick, indicted in 1982 for a variety of complaints relating to his scam, braved the government onslaught, confident that eventually he could win.

The twenty-seven charges against Kirkpatrick were thrown out for lack of substantiation before he could come to trial, and, with all the coldblooded gall of a professional highwayman, the brazen investment counselor attempted to collect on the notes he had swindled his hapless investors into signing.

In 1987, Kirkpatrick discovered just how unforgiving and unforgetting the federal government can be. The Justice Department finally convinced a Denver federal appeals court to reinstate his twenty-seven-count indictment. As even more retribution, the IRS is nipping at his heels and those of his victims.

Kirkpatrick, with all the aplomb of the true con artist, plans to appeal all the way to the U.S. Supreme Court, if necessary.

The African Heir Scam

JOHN ACKAH BLAY-MIEZAH, native of Ghana, along with his American "agent" Robert Ellis, took the rich folks of Philadelphia for an $18 million ride they won't soon forget. Allegedly passing himself off as the royal heir to an evergrowing, $27 billion trust fund ostensibly tied up in Ghana, Blay-Miezah requested financial assistance from many of the top monied people in this country to aid in his fight to acquire what he insists is rightfully his. In return, he offered as much as 1,000 percent return on the loan.

People flocked to the Ghanaian's side—with interest on an investment that high, who wouldn't? Recognizable names float around him—Barry Ginsberg lent him $2 million with a promise of $150 million when the trust fund comes to Blay-Miezah. Word has it that the late John Mitchell, of the Nixon administration, was to receive $733 million for his assistance in steering other money to the Ghanaian.

Too good to be true? TV talkshows, newscasters, pundits proclaim Blay-Miezah a fraud. After all, he's been trying to loosen up his trust fund for over fourteen years now—and living in the overflowing lap of luxury all the while. Heads of governments defer to him, and what if it is true? Why take the chance of missing out on a ridiculously high rate of interest on a small—say, $2 million—investment or losing out on the chance to be cozy with Ghana's new royalty?

Back down on earth, some say the two alleged bunco artists got more than $100 million from their allegedly bogus Ghanaian trust-fund swindle; some say it was closer to $250 million. From 1972 to 1986, they allegedly bled the Pennsylvania bluebloods and the rest of the world nearly dry, taking in $876,150,000. Who knows for certain?

When Blay-Miezah returned to his homeland in a purported attempt to see for himself just where his trust fund stood, the Ghanaians first welcomed him with open arms, then turned on him and slapped him in prison. At one point in this amazing pretender's adventure, he sat on Death Row, waiting to be executed.

But anyone who could sweet-talk tightfisted millionaires into parting with their millions in such amounts as Blay-Miezah allegedly did, could not reasonably meet his end in a Ghanaian prison. Before the ink was dry on the newspapers around the world telling of his death sentence, the Ghanaian heir-to-whatever was out of prison, out of Ghana, and into one of London's most elegant hotel suites and the pockets of some of the UK's wealthiest citizens.

Blay-Miezah presently lives the life of opulent splendor in London, while his partner stews in an American prison, having been convicted of fraud and grand theft. Blay-Miezah would be a cellmate, had he not bolted just in time. And while some people try to disprove the Ghanaian's claims, and American millionaires scream bloody murder about the millions they invested, never to see one penny of return, British millionaires turn a deaf ear and are presently investing heavily in what many insist is a world-class swindle. This story could be classified as unbelievable fiction were it not going on right now.

So You Want to Be In Print?

Going on the theory that most people harbor a secret desire to see themselves in print, CRAIG and TONI SHAW take advantage of people's fantasies by dangling in front of their intended victims an invitation to become published. In city after city, the two scam artists sold advertising space in a nonexistent publication, fleecing would-be writers. For the price of an ad, the investors could have their own column in a proposed new local magazine.

Few small-business owners or hard-working professionals can pass up the offer of relatively inexpensive publicity in a slick regional magazine, especially when that offer includes an in-depth article about their business or a related subject, with their own byline on the piece if they help write the first draft.

Never mind that they have never written before, never mind that they can't write at all. A professional editor, they are told, will smooth off the edges and make their piece truly readable.

From a boiler-room phone setup, the tall, handsome fortyish blond college graduate and his fiftyish petite brunette high-school-dropout partner—along with other phone personnel—called every business listing in the local phone directories, plus leads from everyone already advertising in other magazines, newspapers, throwaway papers, and local ad magazines.

Using an extremely persuasive soft sell, the platinum-tongued Shaws offered advertising space in a proposed upscale regional magazine, telling the pigeons on the other end of the phone just what they wanted to hear:

"Our exciting new ninety-six-page, full-color monthly magazine devoted to the people of this area will be sold on the racks in all supermarkets and 7/Elevens, as well as on newsstands and in all the bookstores." The con artists, very relaxed and sure of themselves, work slowly, their sales pitch growing friendlier by the minute. "And we plan to send out free copies to all waiting rooms in the county—doctors, dentists, shrinks. An ad in our proposed magazine will be seen by everyone."

They know just what their potential victims want to hear and continue their spiel at a controlled pace, never rushing the listener. "This is just what your area needs, and we're shooting for a fifty-thousand minimum print run at first and a readership of at least 250,000 to start."

During the casual and progressively more chummy phone calls, Craig or Toni comment on the wealth of knowledge each prospective ad buyer possesses.

"You know, I just got an idea," they say, as

if just having a revelation. "I hope you won't find it too farfetched, but our magazine could definitely use someone with your background to write an article on your area of expertise. Wouldn't it be great to let our readers know more about how you do your work!"

If the potential victim sounds the least bit interested, the flimflammers press on, suggesting that—"if the editor agrees"—the advertiser just might have his or her own monthly advice column on the subject. If the sucker still hasn't agreed to fork over money for an ad, the Shaws offer to print "the columnist's" photo with the column, along with a short bio and byline.

If the fish passes up the bait and shows no inclination to be published and has a high vanity threshold—although few people can turn their backs on having a byline and their picture and bio in a slick regional magazine—then the Shaws try another tack:

"I understand how you feel. After all, not many people can or like to write; but your company [service, ability] is too intriguing. I tell you what . . . if you buy ad space in our new magazine, we'll send over an associate editor to interview you and write an in-depth article about your business—complete with photographs. I'm sure you could use that kind of advertising—and it doesn't even look like advertising."

The moment the sucker agrees to buy ad

space, Craig or Toni immediately send a runner—some impressionable high-school kid earning a few bucks per day while dashing around town in the bosses' Porsche with car phone—to pick up the payment in advance and "make arrangements" for the ad and the article. Thousands of dollars in checks and cash funnel in daily, while ad copy, photo negatives, and first-draft articles pile up in heaps on the boiler-room floor.

After buying ad space, a cosmetic surgeon is interviewed for an article about the controversy over plastic surgery board certification; he eagerly supplies a number of before-and-after shots of patients. A veterinarian writes a fascinating, if amateurish, article about how to tell if your pet bird is sick, since most birds mask illness to avoid attrition. The piece can easily be rewritten.

An attorney writes an informative treatise on Small Claims Court; a psychologist tells how people need compliments; a hypnotist writes stiltedly about will power; a computer expert gets her own column on understanding bytes, as does a customer who's an expert on astrology. Instead of being paid for their expertise, the suckers pay the Shaws for the privilege of being in print—each advertiser paying a different amount . . . whatever the Shaws can talk them out of . . . anywhere from $100 to $5,000 per ad.

Since the Shaws aren't legitimate, they can

feel out their victims and name their own figures—dickering and sometimes bartering. Instead of cash for ad space in the magazine, the charismatic Shaws are perfectly willing to accept meals at restaurants, large tabs for drinks and entertaining at taverns, clothing from small boutiques and specialty shops, video and stereo equipment, limousine rental, and services of all sorts, from hairstylists to manicurists to electricians.

One boutique after another eagerly provided Toni with size-six clothes purportedly for the magazine's fashion spread. One store provided eveningwear, while another gave her afternoonwear, and still another offered swimwear. A local sports hero traded sneakers and other sports togs from his sports shop in return for a large ad and an article on choosing the correct track shoes. The store owner felt most fortunate, because the Shaws accepted only enough merchandise to pay for half the "going rate" for six months' worth of ads.

Of course, the Shaws' "going rate" was whatever the mark on the other end of the phone was willing to pay. The phone team started out high and allowed themselves to be talked down in price. For a touch of authenticity, the crafty Shaws kept their rates competitive with other publications in the region. Most victims paid between $500 and $1,000 per ad—upfront and in cash or by check—sometimes buying six months' space for a "really reduced" rate. The Shaws took in tens of thousands a week on their scam.

In the late 1980s, Craig and Toni leased a large house in a lovely canyon in the Los Angeles foothills, paying the realty company only the first month's rent along with the promise of a full-page ad and a real-estate advice column in every issue of their new magazine in lieu of monthly rent. They acquired a storefront office the same way. A used-furniture store owner supplied them with desks, chairs, and file cabinets on the promise of free ad space and an article on furniture refinishing; and a used-car dealer advanced them an older-model Porsche complete with car phone in exchange for ad space and his own column on car upkeep. The Shaws also acquired an electric typewriter, copy machine, and office coffeemaker on empty promises.

To the Shaws' consternation, the astrologer innocently brought in a professional editor, forcing the bunco artists into going through the motions of putting together a real magazine.

The astrologer, ecstatic about having her own column but faced with a case of terminal writer's block, contacted a close friend, Joyce Mintz, who had a name in the publishing world as both an editor and a freelance writer. After helping the astrologer through her crisis, Mintz asked if the new magazine needed a theater or restaurant critic. The astrologer gratefully gave her a number to call.

Craig "interviewed" the editor for a position as staff theater critic, sent her out to a local playhouse that evening to review the show, and then "hired" her when she handed in a sparkling review. Putting on a good act for her, the con artists discussed their upcoming editorial meeting—"what with the production deadline just three weeks off"—but were stuck when she asked to attend. Now they had to have that meeting, so they roped one of the phone salesmen and a neighbor into acting as managing editor and art director and put on quite a display for the benefit of the editor and the printer they had yanked at the last minute from the phone book.

Craig found Mintz's resume rich with national-magazine experience—but the young woman had yet to progress beyond senior editor. During the staged editorial meeting, Mintz found herself correcting everyone, losing patience with their obvious inexperience. Craig and Toni knew what they were doing—uncanny at sensing people's weaknesses. Craig stopped the orchestrated editorial meeting, grabbed his jacket, and headed for the front door.

"Let's take a walk," Craig said, opening the door for the editor, who threw on her coat to protect against the January coolness and followed him out onto the sidewalk. "I have a proposition for you." As they strolled down the street, where they could speak freely without being overheard, Craig's tone changed from businesslike to respectful yet friendly. "You have talent—I can tell. You're just what Toni and I have been looking for! We're new at this—admittedly novice publishers. Without you, this magazine might fold, but with you, it's a definite hit!"

The editor liked what she heard.

"Now, before you answer, please think. Toni and I want you, but we can't afford you. Once we get the magazine on its feet, of course, we'll be able to pay you what you're really worth." When the editor smiled, he knew he had her. "I'm going to all but insult you—but think before you say no." His grin disarmed her. "We can only afford to pay you a paltry five hundred a week for the first issue—on a freelance basis as an independent contractor. And you're really going to have to work for it, since the deadline for the first issue—the February issue—is only three weeks away. After that, we'll bring your salary up to where it should be, at two thousand a week on a salary basis."

She opened her mouth, but he continued, "And we'll throw in a thousand-dollar cash bonus when the February issue hits the stands—and add another five hundred a week to your two-thousand-dollar salary after the March issue as our thanks for your patience. In fact, we'll raise your weekly salary in five-hundred-dollar increments with each issue until you're getting four thousand a week. I'm sure our investors will agree to that. Whatd'ya say?"

Dazzled by the title of editor-in-chief and her first opportunity to head up a regional magazine, Mintz was more than happy to wait four or five weeks for a commensurate salary. In fact, she would have accepted even less just for the opportunity to show the world she really could put together a major publication. She started work the next day, and the Shaws had their fall guy for when the magazine folded. They even called their attorney to have Mintz made a one-third partner, but she turned down that offer, knowing that one-third of the profits becomes one-third of the debts should the venture fail.

Unfortunately for the Shaws, the unsuspecting editor didn't know the meaning of the word *failure* and frustrated them constantly by sidestepping the stumbling blocks the scam artists repeatedly threw in her path. When the managing editor—who was actually only a phone salesman—quit, Mintz took over as managing editor. When the inexperienced art director also quit under pressure, Mintz undertook that position, too. With the aid of one young gofer who had a little art training, she ramrodded the magazine, wrote and rewrote all the copy, took the ads and the copy to the typesetter, proofread all the galleys, pasted up the boards herself—working with little food and no sleep for two solid days and nights—

and finally, on schedule, brought the boards to the printer in the company limo, for which the Shaws had bartered.

The Shaws suddenly had a magazine—the last thing in the world the hustlers expected or wanted. Just as in the Zero Mostel-Gene Wilder comedy *The Producers*, where two swindlers intentionally sell well over 100 percent of the project to investors and purposely put on the worst possible musical comedy to create a flop so they could claim a loss and keep the investment cash from so many investors, the Shaws planned to shrug their shoulders and contend they had tried to put out a magazine but everyone on the staff had quit or fouled up. They could chalk it up to inexperience and insist that every penny they took in had been spent on trying to put out the magazine. Under the law, as long as they *tried*, they had committed no crime.

The Shaws, however, hadn't let Joyce Mintz in on their scheme, since she was just one of the suckers they had conned and was to be left holding the bag when they finally split. Unfortunately for the Shaws, the magazine's boards were at the printer. Frantically, the con artists called the printer and canceled the promised 50,000 copies on slick paper, asking him instead to print the least number of copies on the very cheapest paper—1,000 copies on newsprint. Although they refused to pay the typesetter, citing any number of reasons, they were forced to pay the printer, since refusal would indicate a lack of intent to produce a product.

Greedy, the Shaws stalled Mintz on her salary, paying her erratically, every ten days or so, explaining that funds were tight, but once the first issue was out, they could sell more ads and would then pay her $2,500 per week, plus fringes.

When the forty-eight-page February issue came out—in February—the Shaws were astounded. The editor had pulled the job together, putting out a professional publication. She had called her well-known writer friends and asked them to contribute pieces for her without pay to help her get the first issue off the ground. An award-winning author even donated an original short story. Determined to make a go of the magazine, the editor—in her position as managing editor—had also steamrolled the typesetters. When one of the two people working the new computerized typesetting equipment proved incapable of withstanding the pressure of a brutal deadline with accuracy, he quit and walked out. Undaunted, the editor took his place and set type alongside the typesetting company's owner. Working through the night into the next morning, the two completed the type setting on time.

Mintz knew nothing about the minimum print-run of only 1,000 copies and was told the printer had fouled up by using the wrong paper stock. Everything would be made right for the March issue. Mintz immediately started work on the next issue, not worried that her salary hadn't escalated to $2,500 weekly. And the Shaws, who now had a handle on their gullible editor's personality, explained that because the printer had mistakenly used newsprint instead of slick paper, many advertisers were pulling out since the magazine was far from the professional publication they had been promised. The Shaws led Mintz to believe that ad sales—the backbone of any publication—would have been better had she not produced such a shoddy premiere issue.

The Shaws' only out-of-pocket expense besides the first month's rent for their house, which they readily paid, had been the deposit on the three business telephones, personal home phone, and car phone. Knowing they would not be around long enough to be caught by the phone company, they ran up astronomical phone bills. Just before the phone company shut off service for nonpayment of three months' bills, the Shaws picked up and moved two miles away through a new realty company and started up phone service under another name. Unless the police moved in sooner, every three months the con artists changed names and locations, keeping one step ahead of the law and their pigeons.

This time, they worked out of their home with only one extra person on the phones, since the area they could fleece rapidly dwindled as they covered more and more territory. They no longer needed the editor, because they had one thousand copies of a tangible magazine to use as a selling piece and had no intentions of putting out a second issue. They could use the sample magazine to milk every last drop from the San Fernando Valley.

Convinced of the Shaws' sincerity—hadn't she been to their house many times for dinner and treated as one of the family?—the editor had no reason to doubt them. So when she dropped by their home over the weekend, she expected anything but a completely vacant house. As she stood in the empty living room, a young fellow walked in, picked up some houseplants, and headed out the door.

"Can I help you?" he asked on his way in for a second load of plants.

"I'm looking for the Shaws . . ."

"They've moved. I'm taking their plants to them. Follow me." He hopped in his car with the editor on his tail.

When the Shaws saw Mintz, their faces blanched, then almost instantly reacted with feigned pleasure. They greeted her warmly and explained that because the problem with the February issue's paper, they had had to lower their living standards. Her fortuitous visit saved them the trouble of calling her to let her know where they were. She believed them and they wondered why the fates kept tossing this young woman in their way.

They explained they would not be able to pay her the full amount they had promised and would understand if she preferred to accept another position elsewhere. She agreed to hang in for the next issue at the same $500 per week until she produced a decent issue and ad sales picked up. What she didn't know was that sales skyrocketed with the February issue as a sample sales promotional piece. With something to show potential customers and a well-known name as editor-in-chief, and exciting stories and articles, the Shaws sold ad space with renewed vigor and phenomenal results.

For the March issue—which "ad-sales delays" forced to become the April, and then the May issue—the editor hired a close friend who was a veteran art director. She also interviewed the top local TV weathercaster for a feature profile, and then hired a national radio talkshow host to write a sports column. The clever Shaws gave the editor carte blanche, since they planned to take off soon with all the spoils. As long as they could keep putting off the next issue's publication date, they were all right.

When the copy for the second issue was ready—the magazine was now seventy-two pages—and the fashion spread with professional models and fashion photographer was to the editor's satisfaction, Mintz took everything to a new typesetter, one she had interviewed and felt assured could handle the job. So far as she knew, the Shaws and the old typesetter were still at odds about the February issue's disputed bill.

Feeling expansive, with their names on the magazine's masthead as publisher and associate publisher, Craig and Toni acted their roles. When the gofer went for coffee or snacks, Craig always handed him a twenty and told him to keep the change. If the group got hungry, he'd hand out a fifty or a hundred for burgers or pizza. Unfortunately, the Shaws got a little careless. In a magnanimous gesture of overconfidence, on a Thursday, they gave the editor two blank checks with which to pay the typesetter and printer on Saturday. Considering Mintz as more pathetically honest than most of their suckers—who would have jumped at being a one-third owner of the magazine—the Shaws instructed the editor to fill in the amounts on the blank checks only after the work was completed.

By now, the wily Shaws had plucked the entire San Fernando Valley clean and knew it was time to move on to greener sources before the bunco squad nabbed them. They planned to close out their checking accounts Friday and be long gone before the blank checks and the editor's paychecks were cashed.

The galleys would be ready Saturday, and the printer—who insisted on a payment upfront—would start the print run Monday morning. But a number of the galleys were ready early, so the art director and the editor pasted up the boards early Friday at the typesetters. With very little left to do, Mintz filled in the blank check for the full amount and paid the typesetter so he could get to the bank before it closed. Having heard about the problems with the previous typesetter, he took the check straight to the Shaws' bank and asked for cash.

The editor also gave the new printer a check as an advance on the work, which he too took to the Shaws' bank and cashed. Craig and the typesetter crossed paths in the bank but didn't know each other. The printer, also in one of the long Friday-afternoon lines, waved hello to Craig as he cashed Craig's check, and the con artist could do nothing but smile wanly as he withdrew everything else and closed out the account. The only one not to be paid turned out to be the editor, who trusted her employers and deposited her paychecks into her own checking account. Some weeks later, her account showed a shortage for the two paychecks written on a closed account.

Just before the police swooped down on the Shaws for paying salaries with bad checks, the couple held a home sale. They knew the cops were poised to pounce, but true to their trade, the con artists had one trick left up their sleeve. Playing on everyone's sympathy by telling them that their venture into publishing had failed, the Shaws invited the entire neighborhood to purchase their belongings, some very expensive pieces. People flocked to buy their piano and solid-wood furniture, TVs and stereo, and kitchen appliances. The Shaws readily accepted their checks and cashed them all early Monday morning.

That afternoon, with tears in their eyes, Craig and Toni approached each buyer, saying they just couldn't stand to part with their heirlooms and offered "a little extra above the original price" for their trouble. The cunning Shaws bought back everything they had sold—paying with checks from the account they had already closed—and skipped out during the night, beating the police by five hours.

Craig and Toni Shaw remain at large, with warrants out from New York and California. They walk that thin legal line between publishing a magazine and fleecing the public.

CHAPTER 6

Sensational Scalliwags

The Father of Pyramids

CHARLES PONZI, considered the father of the pyramid scheme, didn't invent "the Ponzi." While he may not have thought of the scam first, he ran the swindle so well that it has been called the Ponzi ever since. Originally called Peter-to-Paul, the pyramid scheme was the brainchild of turn-of-the-century Brooklyn bunco artist William Franklin Miller, who first implemented the con game by actually paying off his original investors with money collected from later suckers. Miller's scam proved fruitful, but Charles Ponzi of Boston made it downright famous.

In 1919, Charles Ponzi, fresh out of Canadian prison, opened offices as investment counselor in Boston and told potential investors he would double their money within three months. His plan, he explained, was to buy postal coupons in foreign countries, where they sell for much less than elsewhere, and then bring them to America and sell them for a much higher rate.

The profits would be enormous, the bunco artist promised, and Charles Ponzi was willing to pay his investors well. They complied, handing over their hard-earned cash. Within ninety days, he presented them with double their initial investment—straight from the pockets of new investors.

When word of this remarkable proposition got out, people flocked to Ponzi's offices to buy in. In fact, things went so well that Ponzi even lowered the number of days to the fruition from ninety to forty-five. To pay off these investors, he gave the original investors the money he took from later investors—robbing Peter to pay Paul—and proving to everyone that he was honest and his plan a good investment.

Once the public was set up, he could pocket the money as the scheme came to an end. In the meantime, the one-time clerk became a millionaire, earning as much as $200,000 a day. The man is hailed by many as "the greatest Italian of them all!"

A year later, a reporter with the *Boston Globe* exposed the scam for what it was, and Ponzi experienced a run on his offices—and he paid off $15 million of the $20 million he took in during his first year. Arrested, he spent four years in Plymouth Prison. The last that was heard of Charlie Ponzi was in 1925. Out on appeal, he fled to Florida and started up a real estate scam.

Although the rakish flimflammer may no longer be alive, his name will live on forever in tribute to the greatest swindle of its sort ever pulled.

Private Eye with a Twinkle

GASTON BULLOCK MEANS—considered "the greatest natural detective ever known" by his employers with the Burns Detective Agency—was able to boldly work some of the biggest confidence games of the early twentieth century because of his profession as detective.

Leaving the Burns Detective Agency in 1915, the thirty-five-year-old dimple-faced Means became a private detective, using his reputation as a sleuth to swindle his clients. In 1917, Means gained the confidence of eccentric young heiress Maude R. King, became her manager and protector, and ultimately bilked her of $150,000.

To meet the ditzy young woman who had married a millionaire fifty years her senior and had become a bereaved but immensely wealthy widow four years later, Means set up an almost foolproof situation. He hired a vicious-looking man to mug Maude and her escorts. During the mugging, the private detective—a suave southerner from North Carolina—attacked and ran off the mugger, thus endearing himself to the rich young flapper.

With his background as a former cotton broker and part-time lawyer, Means became Maude King's manager. He manipulated her money and dipped into it so often that even she became suspicious. He then suggested they go for a hunting trip to his old North Carolina homestead—where he lured her into the woods and quite probably shot her dead in cold blood.

For the benefit of local friends and neighbors, he staggered from the thicket, sobbing and bleating that Maude King had shot herself while fiddling with his gun. He explained to any who would listen that he had stopped at a pond and had placed his twenty-five-caliber Colt automatic handgun in the crook of a tree while he kneeled at the creek's edge for a sip of fresh water.

To his horror, he looked up to see his lovely but giddy young employer twirling the gun playfully. He yelled an admonition, startled her, and she dropped the gun—which he claimed went off and shot her just behind the left ear. Not everyone believed his accidental-death explanation, and Means found himself indicted for murder.

He described his shock and consternation in detail for the good ol' boy jury at his trial, and he carefully interjected into his statements a great deal of white supremacy prattle, playing to the predominately Ku Klux Klan jurors. With the tongue of a true con artist and a feel for what the Klan members wanted to hear, Means not only received a verdict of "not guilty," but convinced them to determine that Maude King's death was a suicide!

His escapades during the First World War were straight out of a British spy farce. Representing himself as a master detective and master spy, Means conned the British into hiring him to spy on the Germans. Then he went to the Germans, told them he was a British spy, and offered them his services. They hired him to embarrass the British. Not satisfied with two well-paying employers, he took on another client, the U.S. Army Intelligence Service. The swindler looted and plundered to his heart's content until the war—regrettably, to Means—concluded.

After the Great War, his former employer, William J. Burns, contacted Means and told him there was a strong possibility that Burns might be named as head of the U.S. Bureau of Investigation—forerunner of the FBI—and if he got the job, he wanted Means to work under him. To ensure the outcome, Means surreptitiously used his investigative powers to find all the skeletons in Washington. He blackmailed enough congressmen into writing letters of recommendation to secure Burns's appointment.

One of Means's most daring scams involved blackmailing President and Mrs. Harding. While working as special agent for the Bureau of Investigation, Means discovered that the President was enjoying an extramarital affair. Realizing that the notoriety would be ruinous to the President's career, Means threatened to go public if not paid $50,000. Unfortunately for Means and his scheme, Harding died in office before paying up; but Mrs. Harding came across with $35,000 to keep the corrupt detective quiet.

Means, always enterprising, went to the President's paramour and helped her write a book about her love child with Harding. Means went even further and wrote a book about the President, insinuating Mrs. Harding had poisoned her husband, The book, *The Strange Death of President Harding*, became a bestseller, and Means moved his wife and son into a luxurious three-story white-brick house in one of Washington's more fashionable neighborhoods.

The confidence man's fortune grew as he hired himself out as a master detective. He used a ploy similar to his method of arranging to meet Maude King: he sent anonymous death threats to people and then offered his services to rid them of their unknown enemy. Hoodwinking one millionaire after another, Means capped off his illustrious confidence career by giving Evalyn Walsh McLean, wife of the *Washington Post*'s publisher, a run for her money.

Means took great delight in taking the newspaper magnate's wife for over $104,000 when she naively hired him to find the kidnaped Lindbergh baby. Although he assured his client he'd return the baby to his parents, Means not only never produced the baby, he got away with Mrs. McLean's money. Furious, the woman had the detective prosecuted, and he received a fifteen-year sentence.

Means died in Leavenworth with a smile on his face, refusing to tell where he'd hidden his loot.

Ahead of His Time

STANLEY E. ADAMS, former president of the Lamar Savings and Loan Association of Texas, applied in 1984 through first the state savings and loan commissioner and then the state attorney general's office for permission to open a new branch of his S&L. The attorney general's office stated that Adams's request appeared to be much too "speculative" and summarily rejected it.

Just how speculative could a new branch of an existing savings and loan association be? It would depend, of course, on the location of the proposed branch. The reason for Adams's rejection may have been that his new branch was to be *on the moon.*

In a detailed, well-worded proposal, the then savings and loan president explained how and why he wanted to secure permission for a branch office on the moon and described the area as " 'outer space, including the Moon and other celestial bodies,' as these terms are used in the Treaty of Principles Governing the Activities of States in the Exploration and Use of Outer Space, including the Moon and Other Celestial Bodies."

To allay anyone's fear that this branch might not be easily accessible, Adams proposed that the moon branch be located within the United States lunar base, somewhere within a one-half mile radius of the base. Because such a location could prove temporarily inaccessible, the S&L president requested the commissioner—on a onetime waiver—substitute "astronomical unit" for "mile."

Because an AU equals 92,907,000 miles, the proposed branch could temporarily be set up near NASA's Space Center in Houston, where a Lamar S&L branch already existed. Once the moon is populated, the branch could be moved to its proper lunar location.

Stanley Adams has plenty of time to think up new locations for new endeavors, because in 1988 Lamar Savings and Loan became insolvent and was seized by the Federal Home

Loan Bank Board. Adams is currently under indictment on fourteen counts of fraud.

Star-Studded Stunt

N. JAMES ELLIOTT, a notorious confidence man with a vivid prison record, gained access to a number of famous Hollywood stars. With the smooth tongue of a professional swindler, he conned big-name movie stars into unwittingly working his scam for him.

Elliott, explaining that he needed celebrities for the promotion on his vastly rich silver mine, offered the stars shares in the project if they would go along with him. In a town filled with press gimmicks and publicity ploys, his plan seemed perfect—and quite reasonable to actors already accustomed to publicity. He planned to promote interest and the sale of stock in his [nonexistent] America Silver Mine by hiring twenty Hollywood film stars whose names were all but household words to take turns driving a ten-ton truckload of silver from his mine in Panamint, California, cross-country all the way to Wall Street.

Comedy actor Ben Blue and leading actor Rod Cameron actually showed up to drive the truck. Superstar Errol Flynn wired his regrets; sincerely disappointed, the film swashbuckler wanted to join in but was too ill at the time to make the trip.

The only catch—there was no mine and no silver. But the movie stars didn't know that and, interested in the project and more than happy to do their part for such a strange stunt, most regrettably found their schedules conflicted. Because not enough celebrities turned up, Elliott called off the stunt. Had more big names showed up, there would have been a truckload of Technicolor faces blushing brightly as Elliott pocketed the loot, cast himself as the Invisible Man, and vanished.

How Many Is Too Many?

GIOVANNI VIGLIOTTO, a modern-day Don Juan, racked up 105 wives before one finally hunted him down and put him behind bars. Preying on lonely and vulnerable women of varying ages, the suave bigamist married one women after another—without benefit of divorce from the previous ones—and then suggested he and his new bride move nearer his home, which he always claimed to be somewhere far out of state. He would tell her he could hardly wait to show her off to his family.

Vigliotto talked each new bride into selling her house and packing up most of her belongings. He convinced the bewitched bride that it would be easier on both of them if he were to cart off the belongings in a U-Haul to their new home while she stayed behind to tie up loose ends. For protection, he would also take the money, because a fragile woman alone could be too vulnerable.

It all seemed to make sense at the time, and each of 106 women packed up everything she owned and handed over everything she had accumulated over a lifetime, along with the contents of all her bank accounts, to her attentive and thoughtful bridegroom. Looking forward to the time when she would start up their honeymoon with her smooth-talking husband, she waited for him to call with the exact location of their new home.

When each gullible bride finally became impatient enough and headed for their love retreat, she came up empty. No matter how hard she tried to find her loving groom, she found only that she had been taken. In most cases, the embarrassment proved too much, and the duped bride even refused to call the authorities or press charges.

Bride number one-oh-six, however, had a shorter fuse than the rest and decided to find her missing bridegroom no matter what. She remembered that she had met him at a flea market where he had an impressive amount of choice belongings to sell. He had started up a conversation with her, and she had found him quite interesting and understanding. In a matter of days, he had convinced her that they were getting no younger and should marry.

This woman scorned felt Vigliotto would probably follow his pattern—peddling her belongings at some flea market somewhere while romancing another potential bride. With nothing but vengeance on her mind, she packed up what little she had left and drove from state to state, following the major flea markets. She covered several states before she finally found Vigliotto in a flea market in Florida, selling her belongings.

The vengeful bride called the authorities, had her Lothario arrested for theft and bigamy, and was not the least bit surprised when most of his "brides" refused to press charges and wanted him back.

Parisian Ice Follies

World-famous Parisian jewelers JACQUES and PIERRE CHAUMET found themselves skating on such very thin ice in their business dealings that they finally found a hole and fell in. The Frenchmen—plump, balding brothers in their early sixties—came from an extremely long line of renowned jewelers. The brothers' ancestors provided exquisite gems for Europe's noblest blood; nine generations of Chaumet jewelers of Place Vendôme in Paris kept the wealthy of Europe in sparkling baubles—a reputation to be envied. Their family—one Chaumet after another—took great pride in its history rich with the crowns of royalty dating back to Charlemagne.

In the late 1970s, as the price of diamonds dizzily spiraled upward, *les frères* Chaumet thought it might be a good idea to corner the market on ice. The only flaw in their otherwise brilliant plan was their lack of solid funding. To buy up as many investment-quality rocks as possible at a reasonable price, they borrowed from anyone and everyone, going deeper and deeper into debt on a speculation they considered a sure thing.

By 1985, however, the bottom cruelly fell out of their investment when the price of diamonds plummeted an unprecedented 80 percent, from $48,000 per carat to $12,000. Both Jacques and Pierre panicked and dashed around, clandestinely borrowing more money from their friends and clients in an effort to cover their growing losses. To coax money from their new creditors, they promised a 20 percent return on the investment—and then, in an effort to encourage more funding, started working the old Ponzi scheme.

Using fresh funds to pay off early lenders, they went to banks to finance their receivables, showing that they had paid off most of their initial creditors. Over a short period of time, the Chaumet brothers, longtime pillars of the French establishment by virtue of their lineage and their company's fine name, sank $120 million in debt. Not only did the brothers allegedly take a gigantic chunk out of the French subsidiaries of American Express Bank and Chase Manhattan, but they also allegedly gouged Morocco's trusting King Hassan II for over $35 million.

Sinking ever deeper into the mire of deception and financial ruin, behind their valued clients' backs the frantic Chaumet brothers—acting more like Tweedledum and Tweedledee than the last in an elegant line of jewelers—privately liquidated gemstones consigned to their company for sale. The brothers pocketed the funds, and the jewels' owners knew nothing of the sale. Bringing humiliation to the family business that had sold to Napoleon, the Chaumet brothers went to jail—arrested for swindling their creditors of nearly $300 million.

Although the Chaumets insisted they were without funds and totally penniless, Chase Manhattan Bank ignored their protests and swooped down on their luxurious town house in the Paris suburbs, removing all its possessions. The courts sold off the Chaumet business assets for a paltry $17 million, leaving creditors chafing and searching for possible hidden funds in Switzerland.

Two unwise men gambled with their forebears' reputation and rock-solid company and found themselves behind prison bars; they might as well have been holding ice cubes in their pudgy pink hands, watching the water drip through their fingers. In the wrong hands, Chaumet Jewelers proved no more sturdy.

World-Class Swindler

EDITH REICH, approaching age seventy and displaying every appearance of someone's benign and gracious grandmother, has been classified by those who know her as one of the world's most corrupt people. Originally from Vienna, she emigrated to the United States in 1971 and made a name for herself as an international trade dealer. The heavyweight companies she negotiated for included Miles Laboratory, Cooper Industries, and Dayco.

Considered an international traveling salesperson extraordinaire, Reich used her powers of persuasion and her knowledge of several languages to earn both quite a comfortable living for herself and an impressive, big-league international reputation. Shuttling back and forth across the Atlantic, she set up deals with companies in the Soviet Union to order from the businesses she represented in the United States. Her American clients paid her hefty commissions to convince Soviet firms to buy from her clients, and she worked hard for her money. The chairman of one of the companies she obtained orders for raved about her abilities, stating that she was "smart *and* shrewd . . . a killing combination."

The raves turned to head shakes when the grandmotherly woman found herself arrested. "I didn't need to do it. I was never greedy. I was just stupid," Reich said of her federal conviction on one count of fraud. Initially arrested for fabricating $120 million in fraudulent orders from the Soviets for Dayco rubber and plastic products between 1979 and 1981, Reich pleaded guilty in 1983 to one count of fraud. She received a five-year sentence in the federal penitentiary.

The judge suspended all but four months of her sentence because she so willingly cooperated with the government in their investigation of the matter. On the other hand, the judge also stipulated that Reich would have to make restitution to Dayco for most of the $13 million in advance commisions the Ohio-based company paid her. So far, Reich has paid back $3 million—about one-third of what she agreed to return.

In the meantime, Reich refused to take her arrest placidly. While cooperating with the authorities, she also pointed an accusing finger at Richard Jacob, Dayco's chairman, and maintained that he thought up the swindle in the first place and enlisted her aid in the illegal operation.

Listed in *Fortune* magazine in 1980 as one of the ten toughest bosses, executive heavyweight Jacob denies the older woman's accusations and points a finger right back, insisting she duped him completely. A reporter from *Fortune* asked Dayco's chairman just how someone of Jacob's corporate stature could be so easily "bamboozled by a woman who looks like your grandmother?"

Richard Jacob responded, "She could probably sell to God."

According to Reich, who tells an entirely different story and maintains that the Dayco chairman is the swindler, Richard Jacob desperately wanted his firm to do business with the Soviets and needed her expertise and connections to gain entry to the right markets behind the Iron Curtain. Records show that Jacob retained the grandmotherly international trader in 1979 to coax orders for Dayco plastic and rubber products from the Russians.

To back his enthusiasm for her abilities and add an incentive, the Dayco executive paid Reich $13 million in advance commissions. But, Edith Reich pointed out, Jacob meant to share in her fraudulent commissions and then became greedy.

When someone found out the orders from the Soviets were mostly fraudulent, Dayco sued for the return of their advance. Reich, taking exception to their attitude, countersued, alleging that Jacob initiated the entire swindle and meant to profit by it himself.

While Reich and Jacob battled in the courts, each incriminating the other, the federal government caught wind of the possible scam and stepped in for a thorough investigation of the matter. Not only the FBI, but the Justice Department, the SEC, the IRS, and the Customs Service took careful note of the Dayco civil proceedings. Investigators from several different branches discovered Reich had a long history of fraud.

Reich could never prove her allegations that Jacob had not only been involved, but started the sting; and the Dayco chairman, then sixty-eight, withstood the withering gaze of the federal investigations.

Champion Money Earner—$100,000 per Hour

The very name MICHAEL MILKEN sends chills through people; grown executives cringe, veteran stockbrokers shudder. One man, not yet forty-five, turns Wall Street pale and the financial world green with fear. Whispers of takeovers and sudden bankruptcy flutter and float. All this because one financial wizard nearly toppled the Street and cared very little for spending the unbelievable amounts of money he amassed.

To Milken—quite possibly the Hemingway, Rembrandt, or Shakespeare of finance—the excitement and the glory came with the chase for fortunes and the fabulously clever deals that created them, not in the amassing or spending of the fortunes themselves. In 1987, Michael Milken broke some kind of record when he earned more in one year than any other individual alive: $550 million, his commission from Drexel Burnham Lambert.

While Milken dealt in trillions of dollars and earned billions in some of his two- or three-year maneuvers, his spending pattern remained quite conservative, which may have rankled some. In fact, Milken to this day lives comfortably but not at all lavishly with his high-school-sweetheart wife and three children in a modest home not far from where he grew up. Unlike Donald Trump, he shuns publicity and opulence, preferring to protect his comfort and privacy from a grasping world.

The former whiz kid of finance grew up in Encino, California, a Los Angeles suburb in the San Fernando Valley. His friends and schoolmates agree that he always had a knack with numbers, which in Milken's case would be a gross understatement. Classified by one writer as the "Rain Man of corporate finance," Milken sees through the most difficult financial problems the way a Mozart sees every note of every instrument in a complicated new musical composition.

After attending the Wharton School in Philadelphia and working a few years in New York City to gain that hands-on experience learned only on Wall Street, Milken returned to Southern California and set up offices in Los Angeles. He offered expert financial assistance, saying, "I think of myself as a doctor. So many companies and people need my help."

Having learned the importance of juggling what became known pejoratively as "junk bonds," by 1980 Milken proved himself the world authority on them. Everyone who was anyone beat a path to this financial genius's door, and he assisted many to earn millions and even billions. Approached by MCI, CNN, Metromedia, and a number of other large firms, Milken financed them.

His fiscal prowess brought him trouble when he financed several corporate raiders who attacked some of the country's biggest businesses—National Can, TWA, Revlon, and Beatrice Products. Not all takeover attempts proved successful, but the robber barons made out like bandits anyway, greedily stuffing their accounts with greenmail.

Milken's commissions on the intended raids made him a billionaire. His comet would still be coursing the financial heavens were it not for a severe wind-shear factor in the form of arbitrageur and corporate raider Ivan Boesky. Milken's dealings in junk bonds came under federal scrutiny, and too many questions about stock manipulation remained unanswered. In 1986, federal authorities thoroughly scrutinized Boesky's practices and indicted him for racketeering and securities fraud. In one of the biggest plea bargains ever, the arbitrageur agreed to pay $100 million in fines and spend just "minutes" in a country-club federal prison—if he sold out Milken.

For all his brilliance, Milken found himself federally indicted on ninety-eight counts of racketeering and securities fraud. He pleaded innocent to all counts, while Drexel Burnham Lambert—indicted along with Boesky—offered a guilty plea. After much dickering, Milken finally pleaded guilty to six criminal counts of fraud and received a ten-year sentence and a $600 million fine payable to the SEC.

At press time, Milken remains free on bail pending possible disclosures that would result in a reduction in his sentence, since his culpability is in doubt.

ZZZZZ Barry Best Scam of All

Wunderkind BARRY MINKOW grew up in an extremely modest section of Southern California's San Fernando Valley. While some youngsters toiled for a small allowance or mowed lawns to put pennies in their pockets, Minkow offered to clean people's carpets and rugs for a fee. He parlayed a few customers into a small business; then he formed a company and hired others to assist him. The imaginative youth found a need and filled it—and before long, he incorporated ZZZZZ Best, a growing concern in the Valley.

The teenage carpet-cleaning genius hit the evening news and most other media when he proclaimed himself a millionaire and president of his own company before the age of eighteen. News of this mind-boggling achievement spread fast, and young Minkow's burgeoning business received free advertising his company could never otherwise afford. Television stations led the way, and newspapers and magazines followed. Minkow's name and company seemed on everyone's tongues, and demand for his services doubled, tripled, and nearly went through the ceiling.

As the world looked on in wonder, Minkow proved he alone had created a thriving business from nothing—no financial assistance from Dad, no behind-the-scenes machinations by Mom. With his parents' genes and an intelligence and maturity far beyond that of other kids his age, who preferred to party, hang out in the mall, or chase after girls, the clean-cut kid from San Fernando Valley aimed at the Dow-Jones.

At a time in the late 1970s and early 1980s, when long hair and rebellion were in, Barry Minkow maintained a well-groomed, adult facade, impressing people still further with his obviously acceptable values. His was indeed a Horatio Alger tale in the making, and everyone loves a winner. The young overachiever bowled people over with his glib tongue and facile mind.

As the young man's reputation for excellent work at a fair price permeated the media, his vast holdings expanded at a breakneck rate. By the age of twenty-one, bombastic Minkow's rising star had become a comet whose trajectory was straight up with never a backward glance. The bright young man headed up a company valued at $140 million on Wall Street. Stockbrokers revered this money maven whose greatest assets were his youth and good-natured enthusiasm.

No longer presiding over a lowly carpet-cleaning business, young Minkow expanded into a new field—working with insurance companies to renovate fire-damaged offices. The hyperactive whiz kid took potential financiers on a tour of beautifully restored offices, and money brokers lined up to invest in the latest scheme.

In mid-1988, Drexel Burnham Lambert rushed in with an offer of a $50-million stock issue, and Minkow's comet soared ever higher, apparently approaching a new galaxy. Unfortunately, what next came to light stunned the world even more than Minkow's blazing beginnings. His entire new company proved to be one fraudulent swindle—faked offices that had never been fire-damaged, forged work orders, bogus bank balances. Barry, me boy—how could you?

Still bursting with the chutzpah that had catapulted him to such great heights, young Minkow alleged that he had naively fallen into the financial grip of the underworld and had been forced against his will into crooked business practices. He explained that when he needed refinancing, he went to people who seemed legitimate on the surface but who turned out to be members of organized crime.

Unable to raise the $1.5 million bail, the boy genius spent the best part of 1988 in jail awaiting trial in federal court for fifty-four counts of racketeering, along with securities, banking, and tax fraud. Mentioning the names of his crime benefactors did not help his cause.

Hometown Boy Makes Bad

Born and raised in Winter Haven, Florida, STEPHEN L. SMITH engendered the townspeople's complete trust and respect. And why not? Everyone knew his family—his father owned a local citrus business and young Stephen had hauled fruit from orchards to packinghouses before going off to school. The hometown boy had gone on to graduate from Stetson University in De Land, just outside Daytona Beach, and take his MBA from the University of Georgia before joining the brokerage firm of Merrill Lynch.

Besides, in a town of fewer than twenty-five thousand trusting souls surrounded by orange groves, a person's word is always good and never needs to be doubted. Most scam artists and swindlers head for Florida's important cities and coastal communities—Miami, Palm Beach, Fort Lauderdale, Tampa, Clearwater Beach—leaving Winter Haven, in central Florida, virtually untouched by major money fraud. Until their homegrown hero took them for a financial ride they will never forget, that is.

Stephen Smith's flimflam could only work in an area where trust came first. After two years with Merrill Lynch, he went into the oil and gas business at age twenty-six. The promising young financier started up SH Oil & Gas Exploration Company and "allowed" a few of his closest friends to invest in his company. He worked the Ponzi scheme so well that he and his wife, Heather, lived in luxury for over eight years before his ripoff brought him down.

Asking each investor to keep the transaction secret, he promised a too-good-to-be-true return on the investment, knowing full well it would be impossible for his victims to keep the secret. At first permitting only friends to invest, as word of the sweet "secret" deal spread, he let in anyone with the money to invest—local businessmen, retired senior citizens, anyone with the price of admission. And, employing the Ponzi method of repaying the first investors with later investors' money, he delivered enormous monthly dividends on each investment—in some cases, as much as 95 percent—which only fueled the flames of investors' desire.

Because the people begging him to allow them invest with his company had never been bamboozled before, they had no reason to check up on Smith or his "corporation." All they knew was that their friends had earned vast sums through him. One person even invested $11 million, anticipating huge returns on his investment. It never dawned on anyone to ask him where Smith's company headquarters and oil and gas wells were located. And with a return on investment so extremely high, not one investor thought to check out the corporation to see if it actually was incorporated—or indeed if it even existed.

In an eight-year period, Smith garnered $137 million from almost four hundred investors. During that time, he paid back over $119 million in dividends. With such immense transactions, he was able to set up lines of credit with a number of local banks and took out loans.

Stephen and Heather (the *S* and the *H* in SH Oil & Gas) lived royally off the fruits of his malfeasance, collecting a dozen luxurious automobiles, including three Aston Martins and a Rolls-Royce for Heather, and traveling by private jet. The couple, known for their show horses, bought property in Florida, Georgia, and South Carolina.

Citizens of Winter Haven felt great pride in their homegrown millionaire whose roots went way back in the community. Most of them prospered from the dividends his company paid them through secret transactions. Their pride turned to shock when someone sent the authorities an anonymous letter detailing Smith's activities.

When the authorities confronted the young millionaire with the anonymous tip that his company was bogus, Smith invoked the name of Texaco, telling how his company had contracts with Texaco and a number of other major oil companies. A quick check with Texaco disproved his claim, since Texaco executives have never heard of Smith or his SH Oil & Gas Company. All the corporations he listed denied any knowledge of him or his firm.

In 1988, the state of Florida indicted Smith on 257 criminal counts of racketeering, securities fraud, and grand theft. While some people realized they had been duped and felt they had been badly used, still others refused to believe they had been hoodwinked and loudly criticized the Florida Comptroller's office for shutting down Smith and his company.

Although Florida acts as a magnet for swindlers and scam artists, drawing the biggest and the best from all over the country and the world, Stephen L. Smith may have made local history. He siphoned off over $100 million from trusting small-town folk. As one of Winter Haven's attorneys said of Smith, "He just told them they'd make money. It was blind trust. When you know a man's parents and grandparents, and he's been here all his life, you ought to be able to trust him."

Winged Victory or Clipped Failure?

Johnny Carson drove one, and so did Marty McFly to get *Back to the Future*. JOHN Z. DELOREAN, of course, created it—the stainless-steel dream car of the future with distinctive gull-wing doors and a sleek-lined promise of tomorrow. The DeLorean made its debut in 1981 with a commensurate price tag of $25,000. Few could afford to own one, but many could fantasize themselves behind the wheel, careening around dangerous curves with the wind whipping and their hearts racing.

A brilliant executive with General Motors, John DeLorean left a promising career with the top company in the auto industry to start up his own business. To finance the initial research and development of his dream car, in 1978 the innovative automaker raised $12.5 million from a very eager group of investors who felt sure they would receive a large return on their investment.

Seeking additional funds for the actual manufacturing in Great Britain, DeLorean received loans and grants from the British government to the tune of more than $120 million. The man who proved even better at securing funding than he was at making automobiles set up the DeLorean Motor Company manufacturing plant in Northern Ireland, where labor was cheap but quality the best.

Even before the sports cars rolled off the assembly line in 1981, DeLorean Motor Company's future looked bleak. While the recession at home could not have hit at a worse time, DeLorean's firm would probably have gone under, anyway. The money just was not there; and DeLorean filed for bankruptcy in 1982, just months after the first car hit the salesroom floor. The concept had been a smash, but the production had faltered, or so it would seem.

Only about nine thousand gull-winged sports

cars ever made it to American roadways. The high selling price, coupled with a recession in the United States, caused potential customers to pull back and wait. But DeLorean couldn't wait and needed supplemental funding. He made what most people consider an error in judgment when he allegedly tried to raise through illicit means the funds desperately needed to salvage his business.

Having depleted all legal avenues of future funding, the foundering automaker allegedly made a last-ditch effort to keep his company from going under and agreed to an illegal means that involved a large amount of cocaine. The deal turned out to be a government sting, and DeLorean found himself arrested and indicted by a federal grand jury on drug-trafficking charges.

While DeLorean went on trial and was found not guilty of the drug charges, his luck had not changed all that much. The federal government, in looking into the automaker's bankruptcy, found more than they had expected. Federal investigators discovered that the then sixty-year-old innovator had allegedly bilked his investors out of $8.9 million. Another grand jury indicted him on charges of mail and wire fraud, interstate transportation of stolen money, and income tax evasion.

From what the federal investigators could piece together, DeLorean's opulent lifestyle proved his undoing. More of the investors' fundings allegedly went into Mr. and Mrs. DeLorean's New Jersey mansion, California ranch, and New York twenty-room apartment overlooking Central Park than into the DeLorean Motor Company.

Most of the investors' research money allegedly went into DeLorean's personal account; some allegedly went to buy a Utah-based manufacturing company that had nothing to do with automobiles, while the rest allegedly went for DeLorean's personal expenses and, ironically, to pay back a loan. But DeLorean passionately denies the charges, emphasizing in his 1985 autobiography, *DeLorean* (Zondervan), that "when all the documents and facts are presented, I expect to be fully vindicated."

In the meantime, the automaker plans to come out with a new version of the gull-winged design with an improved engine and transmission. Seeking investors for his comeback effort, DeLorean remains ever the optimist. An auto company expert with Drexel Burnham Lambert, when asked about the probability of investors seeing a profit, told a *Time* magazine reporter that "it would be more fun to just go out and throw your money off the Brooklyn Bridge."

CHAPTER 7

Group Stings

Grapes of Deceit

WINEGATE, as the world press dubbed the incident back in 1973, came about when eighteen of France's most distinguished wine merchants perpetrated an $800,000 swindle on the world wine drinkers. Why such a simple deception had not been perpetrated sooner is anyone's guess. Opportunity, of course, has always been a factor, but until recently the people of France—and indeed all vintners of quality wines—took pride in their labels and would never consider bilking the world. Obviously, some wine merchants have more pride than others.

The Bordeaux regions, renowned for their special grapes and outstanding wines—Châteaux Mouton-Rothschild, Châteaux Lafite-Rothschild—held a place of honor in the world of wines, producing some of the world's finest Bordeaux wines and most of the world's red wines. But when a recognized commercial enterprise relies solely on the weather for its profits, an exceedingly dry or overly rainy season can produce a small or less than heroic crop. While the quality of the grape remains constant—relying on the soil the vines grow in—the quantity of the grape dips, as does the money it brings in, souring the revenue for at least one year.

In 1973, the wine merchants found themselves with too few barrels of wine from the normally lush Bordeaux region of France, caused by a disappointingly small crop. Rather than swallowing the loss themselves, the merchants banded together—some say under the protection of then Premier Chauban-Delmas and led by the head of the shipping and bottling firm of Cruse et Fils, Frères, Lionel Cruse—and decided to sweeten what would have been a very tart financial year through trickery and deceit.

The respected wine merchants blended large quantities of cheap white wine with smaller quantities of heavy red wine, producing an acceptable red wine that would have stood up to anyone's palate. But they purposely mislabeled their product by virtue of not mentioning the blend at all; blended wines sell for a much lower price than the pure grapes. When someone leaked the news to the media, the duplicity rocked the wine industry, where reputation is far more important than content.

The French government confiscated 1.9 million bottles of tampered blended Bordeaux, impounding also 382,000 gallons of bogus Bordeaux still in the vats. Sadly, Lionel Cruse's family had been in the wine shipping and bottling business since 1852.

The Family That Preys Together . . .

THE "TERRIBLE" WILLIAMSONS, to this day, strike terror into the hearts of their previous victims, as well as law enforcement officials around the country. An inbred multifamily gypsylike clan, the Williamson gang swoop down on a town or a city like a tornado of chicken hawks and pluck at will, counting on the gullibility and greed of the populace to generate the tens of thousands of dollars or more they derive from their victims each week. Employing a variety of swindles—from faulty roof and driveway repair to sloppy house painting or siding—the ruthless Williamsons swarm into an area and quickly fleece an entire neighborhood before moving on to their next site.

The confidence group usually travels by luxury car—Cadillacs and Lincoln Continentals—and trailers or RVs. They prefer to live in trailer parks, where their privacy is ensured. In regions without trailer parks, they rent apartments or houses by the week in the most transient area of town, where few questions will be asked. What they garner from their victims, they split up among themselves, offering up one special share in respect to the head of the clan, who rarely goes on the road and usually stays at home in Ohio, collecting his part of each take from all the groups around the country.

The Williamson family originally came from Scotland, arriving in Brooklyn in 1895, and have terrorized innocent victims in America ever since. Just before the First World War, these inbred confidence people left their first settlement in New York City and took up permanent headquarters in Cincinnati, Ohio. Within their incestuous ranks are the Stewarts, Greggs, Johnstons, Keiths, McMillans, McDonalds, and Reids. An extremely close-knit family, they keep fairly much to themselves.

Considered a "con clan," somewhere between fifty and two hundred family members descend on the unsuspecting people of an area and run their scams on them. After the turn of the century, the Williamsons preyed on housewives, especially those in the more rural areas. Besides offering crude repairs that lasted until the first good rain, they also sold bogus items at expanded prices.

The Williamsons dealt with a couple of reputable New York wholesalers who provided the clan with inferior merchandise to peddle at exorbitant prices. The wholesalers sent the Williamsons' order through General Delivery in each of the family's chosen destinations, mailing them their goods to be picked up on their arrival.

Whether the item for sale was Irish lace or Persian rugs or English woolens or Russian fur coats—purportedly imported and warranteed with fancy brand-name labels—the only real guarantee that came with the merchandise was that it would fall apart before the week was out. By then, however, the con artists would be long gone.

As their numbers grew, the Williamsons' pattern of behavior grew bolder. To this day, they drive into a neighborhood and target one house. For a reasonable fee, they asphalt the driveway or paint the house on this one job with proper materials and do fairly good work. Then they go to the rest of the neighborhood, telling their potential victims that they have supplies left over from the job they just did and can do at least one more driveway or paint one more house for next to nothing, because they'll use the leftover materials from the previous job.

The suckers, rising to the bait, buy the cut-rate offer—as do half the people for blocks around, all of them thinking they're the only one getting the special reduced price. The Williamsons take care to run certain swindles only when the weather's good, because the first seasonal rain washes away the "asphalt" or inferior paint thinned with crankcase oil.

In the Midwest, fake lightning rods proved a good selling item, and barns coated with Williamson paint warped within days. Known as the "Terrible Williamsons" since 1938, when a law-abiding Willliamson cousin wrote a letter to the Pittsburgh Better Business Bureau to expose his law-breaking kin, the flimflamming family can be mean and vicious. When they gather in major areas, fights and death usually follow. Trailer parks where they stop often become battlegrounds for the Williamsons and the other families when they dispute territory or share of take.

Their infamous tactics and pattern of movement across the country are so well known that the law-enforcement agencies in most large cities automatically warn citizens well in advance through the media and try to convince the group to move on. While the Williamson families avoid most of New England, having been jailed there merely for selling without a license, they head to California each year for the climate and the suckers.

More than six hundred family members flood into the Los Angeles basin on a regular basis, as newspapers and TV warn propective victims of the impending financial danger of dealing with the Williamsons. Usually their audacity allows them to enroll their children in public schools in Southern California, as they enjoy the warm weather during the winter season. With California besieged by drought, the con clan need not hurry out of the area, because without rain to wash away their handiwork, few customers notice the fifth-rate work they've paid for until it crumbles or peels.

A Little Culture

CULTURE FARMS, along with Activator Supply, both Nevada-based companies, bilked over thirty thousand people out of their life savings through a clever scheme that offered a grand return on a relatively small investment, and the opportunity of working out of their own homes. Those who bought in first received a good return on their investments; but since it was the old Ponzi scheme at work, relatively few people in the thirty states hit by the swindle got back any part of their initial investment.

The Culture Farms starter kits sold at prices of $395 up, plus shipping and handling, and consisted of nothing more than milk and grated cheese to be fermented, along with a supply of foil envelopes.

All the investor needed to do, after reading

the simple instructions, was to blend the milk and the cheese and then wait for a mold to grow on top. Once the mold appeared, the fungus should be carefully skimmed off the mixture and mailed back to the company in the foil-sealed packets. This mold, the investors were all assured, would be bought back by the company at between $6 and $10 per packet to be used exclusively by House of Cleopatra Secret as the base for expensive cosmetics.

Americans from all walks of life—all sniffing the sweet smell of success and knowing how much money can be made in as lucrative a business as cosmetics—invested heavily in this uncomplicated venture only to find out after they and their investments were parted that the company no longer accepted mold from new investors. Investors across the country found themselves nostril-deep in vats of foul-smelling fungus with no possible market for it.

Film star Jane Powell, duped into being the House of Cleopatra Secret media spokesperson, found herself in a long line of hoodwinked celebrities who innocently advertised a nonexistent product in all good faith and for the usual fee. And some very clever swindlers made off with over $100 million after having stuck their suckers with a lot of stinking mold.

When the heat in the U.S. got too great, Culture Farms and Activator Supply moved their foul-smelling pyramid scheme to Canada, where they presently pander their curds and whey to naive North Americans.

How Do You Say "Pollution" in Italian?

ITALIAN CON WOMEN seized on the tragic disaster and fear of fallout from the terrifying 1980s Chernobyl incident as the perfect swindle to part Mediterranean marks from their lire. A group of confidence women in the major Italian cities of Rome, Venice, Florence, and Milan posed as government decontamination experts as they went from house to house in a search for the poisonous fallout created by the radiation meltdown in the Soviet Union.

Carrying Geiger counters that went off when they turned them on inside the dupe's house, the flimflamming females convinced their victims that they faced a life-or-death situation and had to have a complete decontamination immediately. They then offered to decontaminate the household and all its occupants for a price.

With the extreme terror of deadly radiation that followed the Soviet tragedy, panic outweighed common sense; and people handed over their hard-earned lire to be cleansed of the radioactive pollution within their homes.

Untested War Materials

GENISCO TECHNOLOGY Corporation, a Southern California firm, and three employees of its Transducer Parts Division came under indictment for conspiracy and fourteen counts of making false statements to a government agency. Pressure transducers for the HARM missile, Coast Guard helicopters, and Navy torpedoes were sent out untested; yet the men in charge of these crucial parts created fraudulent records that claimed the company had tested the transducers.

Between 1985 and 1987, Genisco general manager Werner Brinkschulte, supervisor Danny K. Evans, and quality assurance manager Robert L. Kersnick allegedly fabricated test data and certified them. The Pentagon alleges that Brinkschulte ordered the fabrication of test results rather than actually conducting them, Evans created the computer program that fabricated the false data, and Kersnick validated the phony data. The three also allegedly switched serial numbers of the equipment that had been tested and added resistors to make the out-of-specification transducers appear acceptable to a visiting inspector.

The pressure transducer plays a critical role in some of this country's most vital equipment. It is used: as an altimeter on the Texas Instruments AGM-88A HARM missile; to measure engine oil pressure on the U.S. Coast Guard/Aerospatiale HH-65A Dolphin helicopter; and to measure depth on Navy torpedo test equipment.

Found guilty on all counts, Brinkschulte, Evans, and Kersnick are each serving an extended prison term. This criminal fraud cost Genisco nearly $10 million in fines and claim settlements, but more important, could have caused a number of lives lost through faulty equipment, all to save a little time and a few dollars.

GE Doesn't Always Bring Good Things to Life

Best known for its television sets and toasters and other household appliances, General Electric in 1985 was also America's sixth-largest defense contractor. With fully 20 percent of the company's revenues coming from U.S. military funding, the corporation worked hand in hand with the government on a number of projects, including the Minuteman missiles. As this country's ninth-largest industrial corporation, GE enjoys a fine reputation as a quality-oriented American firm.

Unfortunately, in 1985, a few overachieving

executives played kickball with GE's reputation in an attempt to cut costs and make up losses from a fixed-price contract that had gone far over the original estimate. Until the Pentagon unearthed the $800,000 fraud, GE had enjoyed twenty-five scandal-free years.

Whether or not Minuteman missile-work manager Ray Baessler, who admitted wrongdoing, chief engineer on the Minuteman project Joseph Calabria, who denies any guilt, and a handful of other GE managers bilked the Pentagon all on their own or with the blessings of their corporation may never be known, because they are taking the fall for the corporation.

When it became clear that the upgrading of the reentry vehicles for the Minuteman missiles would leave the company knee-deep in red ink on a contract where losses could not be passed on to the customer, someone formulated a plan to minimize the deficit. In light of the $1.04 million criminal fine and $1.08 million civil penalties levied against General Electric, bilking the Pentagon out of $800,000 no longer seems like such a good idea.

To make up their losses, the GE managers falsified workers' time cards without the employees' knowledge. Of course, while GE is not the only corporation to swindle the government, the suspension of permission to bid on future defense contracts puts a large dent in the corporate coffers. But not as large as the hole in the company's reputation.

Chairman of the Board John Welch's open letter to all GE employees says it best: "We've seen, all too clearly, how the actions of a few can hurt an entire company and all of its employees."

CHAPTER 8

Doctored Data

When scientists work long and hard to prove a theory or find a cure, some of them—out of complete frustration or impatience—may be tempted to tailor their data to fit their theory. Few truly dedicated scientists would risk their careers by stooping to publishing fraudulent findings, but not everyone is completely honest.

If someone's research results appear to be too perfect, too good to be true, they may be just that—too good to be true. Some data manipulation may have come into play. History books do not always include the frauds with the findings, and often great hoaxes are punished with a wink and a nod. But if a scientific cheat forged data on medicinal findings, the results could be universally embarrassing, while still others could prove potentially dangerous and possibly lethal.

The Gravity of the Situation

ISAAC NEWTON—known to children the world over as the serendipitous seventeenth-century scientist who snoozed under a fruit tree and discovered one of the world's most important "givens," gravity—was not immune to a little scientific hanky-panky. Few students, however, are taught that a number of those in the scientific world of Sir Isaac's day were privy to the fact that the brilliant physicist, mathematician, and civil servant intentionally "improved" on his calculations while preparing many of his scientific theories, including his law of the earth's gravitational pull.

Most in-depth encyclopedia and biographical studies on Newton point to the man's two nervous breakdowns and his inability to control his emotions. In his day, Newton and his scientific findings were all but obscured by lawsuits of plagiarism, academic feuds, and monumental bickering on a level of viciousness only someone of Newton's probable emotional instability could reach.

While proving gravity exists, Sir Isaac also went a long way in demonstrating that no one is above more than a little petty nastiness—and in Newton's case, a great deal. The scientist did not expand on his work for profit or fame; his was a more pernicious personal reason: to overshadow and discredit contemporary rivals, British scientists Robert Hooke and John Locke and German philosopher and mathematician Gottfried Wilhelm Leibniz—in a frenzy that could only be considered paranoia by today's psychological standards.

Sir Isaac turned anger into blind wrath and ferociously attempted to ruin his competitors—and in some cases, succeeded. A close friend could find himself fighting for his professional life if he even appeared to question Newton. More than one career crumbled under Sir Isaac's mean-spirited machinations within the scientific and academic communities, often from the most innocent provocation. Once Newton became the leader of the scientific community, all others were in his grasp, and he showed no mercy.

Obviously not all heroes of historical import are perfect, and Newton proved the point. If stretching the scientific truths became necessary to accomplish his ends, history shows Sir Isaac Newton stopped at little to crush his contemporaries and prove his points.

The Piltdown Man

In a vast science amphitheater at the University of California in Berkeley in 1955, a full professor of anthropology droned on week after week about one Age of Man after another, almost lulling himself to sleep along with his two hundred students. Not until he came to the 1912 discovery of the Piltdown man did his eyes light up and his voice come to life with a renewed energy.

"The Piltdown man, as you can see from the screen," he boomed, his voice quavering as he pointed to the replicated prehistoric human illuminated on the vast slide projection facing the students, "will go down in history as paleontology's greatest find!" With extreme reverence, the dean of anthropology detailed the possible beginnings of his science's favorite finding.

To him, all other archaeological unearthings paled by comparison, and the professor usually spent the bulk of his allotted lecture time each semester on this rare early-twentieth-century discovery. What science called the Piltdown man was, in the minds of most scientists of the day, the perfect "missing link"—that proven connection between the evolved apes and our rightful human ancestors everyone had sought for so long.

The professor's eyes glistened as he explained how, on the basis of one jawbone and tiny fragments of a skull found in a gravel pit on Piltdown Common near Sussex, England, in 1912, attorney Charles Dawson presented his find to the scientific world as proof of the existence of a human creature predating Neanderthal man. The UC professor's lectures would go far beyond the assigned anthropology text's short partial chapter on the Piltdown man as he read from his own copious study notes. The professor's students all knew of his obsession with this particular prehistoric human and that he viewed "Dawson's breakthrough," as it was known in those days, as vital to science. They also knew that most of the material in their midterm and final exams would focus on their professor's favorite preoccupation, and they could pass his course with good grades by merely boning up on the Piltdown bones.

Functioning as detectives piecing together puzzles, the entire scientific world of anthropologists, archaeologists, and paleontologists worked as the Sherlock Holmes of their day, sometimes jumping to conclusions from the sparsest of clues, with only their peers to keep them honest.

Of course, Dawson's discovery and hypothesis preceded scientific equipment that could prove positively how early such a bone fragment could have existed. Once the scientific world invented carbon-14 dating, whereby anything could be precisely pinpointed in time, answers to theretofore inexplicable questions tumbled forth and leaps of scientific faith suddenly became fact . . . or fiction.

Thus it was that UC professor—along with

many other instructors around the world—found his semester's lecture shortened by many weeks when the Piltdown man's jawbone and skull fragments proved to be anything but the celebrated missing link—and in fact one of the greatest hoaxes ever perpetrated on the scientific community.

The highly controversial discovery of the Piltdown man had polarized the scientific world, with those who accepted the finding as fact enbracing it as the elusive missing link, while others stood on the sidelines and jeered loudly. Without tangible proof, either side could be correct; but the find's existence had been duly noted in the scientific literature and many professors touted the finding to their students.

Hadn't Martin Hinton—UK's Natural History Museum volunteer and expert on the prehistory of the Thames Valley—authenticated it? Hadn't Sir Arthur Keith, one of the world's most eminent anatomists, given the finding his blessing? Why, even theologian Teilhard de Chardin had raised his voice in favor of the Piltdown man's acceptance.

In 1959, however, a carbon-14 dating of the Piltdown skull particles proved the pieces to be recent human fragments, while the jawbone was that of an ape. After much furor in the press, Dawson admitted planting the bones in the Piltdown Common merely for the publicity and limelight. When he began his hoax, he never dreamed he would find himself in history books under F for Fraud.

On the other hand, growing sentiment leads some scientific Sherlock Holmes types to point an accusatory finger at Hinton, Keith, and de Chardin. One of them, or perhaps all three, may ultimately wear the mantle of forger and fraud. Only time will tell.

Kangaroos in Kashmir?

Motives for false claims are not all alike; nor are the reasons for discrediting someone's findings. Prominent East Indian paleontologist Viswa Jit Gupta purports to have discovered certain fossils in the Himalayas that Australian scientist John A. Talent insists could not possibly have been found there. The two distinctly different tiny fossils in question—ammonoids, an ancient mollusk from Erfoud, Morocco, and conodonts, microscopic jaw sections of segmented worms from the Amsdell Creek area of New York State—Dr. Gupta claimed to have found in the stratospheric regions of India and Nepal.

Dr. Talent and Dr. Gupta—at each other's throats for two decades—offer varying theories on the minuscule fossil findings. The Australian, a paleontologist at the Macquarie University in Sydney, insisted that his opponent's dating and placing of the early fossils are sheer "bumkum." Calling Dr. Gupta's findings the "Himalayan hoax," Dr. Talent asserted that the "geology of the Himalayas has been mucked up from one end to the other" by the Indian scientist. The scientist from Down Under pointed out that Gupta's so-called Himalayan findings were so far off, he might as well have claimed rhinoceroses came from Rio de Janeiro or that kangaroos were native to Kashmir.

In his own defense, Dr. Gupta, a professor at Punjab University, declared Dr. Talent to be "far from the truth," and alleged that the Australian's charges are from "malicious bias and professional jealousy." Accusing Talent of lying, Gupta pointed out their twenty years of differences that Talent obviously wanted to cash in on.

While the matter might have remained one man's word against another, a third scientist added his two cents' worth. Gary Webster, a Washington State University geology professor, had coauthored nine scientific papers with Dr. Gupta. When the question of credibility sprang up, Webster checked his documents and came to the conclusion that he had not been wary enough. Upon closer inspection, he decided with complete certainty that the Gupta specimens had to have been found someplace other than the Himalayas.

"As I see it," Dr. Webster stated in extreme

anger, "it leaves every paper Gupta ever has authored in question. He has willfully tried to dupe the scientific community."

The British journal, *Nature*, commented that Dr. Gupta's "Himalayan hoax will cast a longer shadow" than the Piltdown man in Great Britain. In the 1912 incident, the journal pointed out, only one skull proved to be false, and little needed to be expunged. In this case, numerous scientific reports and findings "will be excised from the record only with much greater difficulty."

The highly respected *Journal of the Geological Society of India* officially advised its readers to ignore all research published by Viswa Jit Gupta over the past twenty-one years, thus validating the devastating scandal rocking both Indian and world science.

Many of Dr. Gupta's findings were conveniently located in politically sensitive border areas of India where it would be difficult if not impossible to go to check. Dr. Gupta's response: "Lies, all lies!"

Publish or Perish

ELIAS ALSABTI, an Iraqi-born fraud, created a false persona and conned his way onto the staffs of many U.S. schools and hospitals by plagiarizing articles from obscure scientific publications. From 1977 to 1980, Alsabti stole well over sixty articles from little-known journals and passed them off as his own by rewriting them in his words and sending them off to respected journals under his own name. He cared little about the subject matter, grabbing everything he could from marginal journals, because only his byline mattered.

With this vast amount of published research data in so many different areas under his byline in the respected literature, and sometimes adding a Ph.D. as well as an M.D. after his name, Alsabti cashed in. The apparently prolific research physician became a sought-after medical expert in many fields and easily secured himself solid, if not cushy, medical positions at some of the country's top-flight hospitals, including Houston's Southwest Memorial.

No one questioned the impostor's abilities during his tours of employment, and he might still be practicing medicine in Houston had his plagiarism not been spotted by some of the scientists whose work he stole. As the first complaints came in, Alsabti swiftly disappeared and has never been found.

Using Those Gray Cells

DR. STEPHEN E. BREUNING, assistant professor of child psychiatry at the University of Pittsburgh and academic star before the age of thirty, presented the mental health community with an almost too-good-to-be-true study in the mid-1980s, proving that neuroleptic drugs caused more harm than good in mentally retarded patients. His documented findings, coauthored by a respected scientist, indicated that these patients' IQs doubled when taken off the drugs; welcome news to the medical community.

But Dr. Breuning's colleague Robert Sprague, then director of the Institute for Child Behavior and Developoment at the University of Illinois, viewing the data as suspect because it was just a little too perfect, played detective. Instead of checking and rechecking Breuning's data, Dr. Sprague checked out Dr. Breuning and discovered that the researcher could not possibly have conducted the work he claimed he had. Conclusion: he must have falsified his data.

Had the medical community readily accepted Dr. Breuning's findings and acted on them before Dr. Sprague looked into them in-depth, the results could have been disastrous to mentally retarded patients everywhere. Breuning's phony data "proved" retarded patients didn't need the medications they took—and if some physician removed his patients from their medicinal regimen, the damage might have been far-reaching and quite damaging.

Alarmed, Dr. Sprague called the National

Institute of Mental Health and presented his suspicions. In looking into the matter, it was found that data used to publish a scientific paper on ten mentally retarded youths could not possibly have been gathered by Dr. Breuning at Oakdale Regional Center for Developmental Disabilities. At that time, Dr. Breuning's position at the Oakdale facility permitted him to study only goldfish and rats—no humans.

A panel gathered to look into the matter unanimously found that Dr. Breuning, an NIMH grant-recipient, had "knowingly, willfully, and repeatedly engaged in misleading and deceptive practices in reporting results of research . . ." and "did not carry out the described research." The panel's conclusion: Dr. Breuning "engaged in serious scientific misconduct."

Following the findings of the fraud investigation, the University of Pittsburgh returned to the NIMH the $163,000 in grant money obtained by Dr. Breuning. Dr. Breuning supposedly spent a little over $51,000 of that grant money while working under Dr. Sprague on a project never performed, and a Justice Department criminal investigation is currently under way.

While Dr. Sprague received commendations for having turned in his colleague, the panel questioned Dr. Sprague's judgment for having included Dr. Breuning's unquestioned publications in his progress reports with such an uncritical eye. The panel also expressed distress at Sprague's "failure to adequately oversee" Breuning's work while under his supervision.

For his actions, Dr. Breuning—who produced between 1979 and 1984 fully one-third of all the literature in the psychopharmacology of the mentally retarded—is barred from federal grants for ten years, which some peers view as a mere slap on the wrist. Breuning still conducts his research, without federal aid, but now the medical world looks askance at anything he does.

Test Case

JOHN DARSEE, a brilliant young cardiologist, brought his potentially auspicious career to a screeching halt when he was caught fabricating research data at Harvard in 1981. Of the 109 papers written by the promising heart specialist, 47 carried coauthors. Not until two inquisitive researchers from the National Institutes of Health launched a full-scale investigation did the true extent of Dr. Darsee's deception come to light.

In 1983, Walter W. Stewart and Ned Feder of NIH started a probe into the writings of John Darsee, whose work at the Harvard Medical School laboratories of cardiologist Eugene Braunwald proved fraudulent. The duo discovered that Dr. Darsee had also fabricated data while attending Emory University School of Medicine and as far back as his undergraduate days at Notre Dame University.

Dr. Darsee's papers, stated Stewart and Feder, appeared overflowing with obvious errors and inconsistencies, along with the fraudulent data. With forty-seven coauthors, why had not one of them called attention to Darsee's slip-ups? And why had journal editors and referees also failed to stem the flow of unmistakable errors?

A Father's Love

PROFESSOR GARY L. TISCHLER proved that some fathers' love knows no bounds and can cause total upheaval when good judgment is superseded by that love. As chairman of the Yale Department of Psychiatry and chief of psychiatry at Yale–New Haven Hospital in 1985, Tischler—with the aid of Boris M. Astrachan, director of the Yale-affiliated Connecticut Mental Health Center, and two associates—put his then unemployable twenty-six-year-old daughter Laurie on an annual salary of $14,000 as psychiatric consultant of the state mental health center.

Laurie Tischler, who had been physically and emotionally debilitated by a series of serious operations over a four-year period, could not secure a paying position for herself. The closest she came to actual employment was to donate her time to a private facility with no connection to Yale or the state mental health facility. Her concerned father, abetted by his associates, created the consulting position and made sure his daughter received a monthly paycheck. Laurie did no consulting.

Dr. Tischler and his friends falsified records and forged contracts in an attempt to justify Laurie's paychecks. A routine state audit brought the "impropriety" to light, and a flurry of resignations and demotions followed. The center's administrator and his assistant lost their positions and received suspensions on their appointments as lecturers at Yale Medical School. Drs. Tischler and Astrachan resigned their administrative positions but remained as professors of psychiatry.

It Takes One to Know One

For more years than he would care to count, forty-nine-year-old, renowned Canadian psychiatrist SELWYN SMITH, M.D.—Royal Ottawa Hospital's psychiatrist-in-chief—had been called on to testify as an expert witness at hearings and trials of defendants accused of white-collar crimes. In the literature and in interviews in popular magazines, Dr. Smith declared the typical white-collor thief to be someone from a better-than-average background who is a high-achieving workaholic with an excellent work record.

The scientific community embraced Dr. Smith's psychological profile of this type of criminal, looking to him as an authority in the field. Unfortunately, members of the Royal Ottawa Hospital's Associates of Psychiatry—the hospital's forty-three-member psychiatric organization—now classifies Dr. Smith as falling into the category he so expertly described.

The Australian-born Dr. Smith had served as chairman of the Associates since 1978, having joined the Royal Ottawa Hospital staff in 1976. Suddenly and without warning, in 1987, the hospital fired the psychiatrist just as the authorities arrested him and charged him with misappropriation of funds from the Association. Almost simultaneously, the Association launched a civil suit against their former chairman to regain the $398,000 his colleagues insist he embezzled from them.

In his denial of any wrongdoing, Dr. Smith said, "It must have seemed like great stuff—here's a guy who writes about something and then gets caught up in the same kind of thing." In a sworn affidavit, the psychiatrist pleaded his case and insisted he was innocent of all charges. He asserted that the hospital agreed that he should receive about $100,000 annually for his administrative duties, and he had paid income taxes on the sum.

Although his total assets—well over a half-million dollars—were frozen pending litigation, a district court judge finally released Dr. Smith's $54,000 Jaguar and a little over $10,000 in stocks. Without a staff position, the psychiatrist returned to private practice, his income sorely curtailed.

Dr. Smith can only wonder that the treatment he received was very similar to that of the white-collar workers he profiled and thus achieved so much publicity. The media coverage apparently hurt more than anything else. The psychiatrist said of the media, "The reporting has been quick and dirty."

Before they even get into court, civil and criminal cases of all kinds are presently being tried in the media as TV and radio stations and the print media do their little dance of attempting to scoop one another to the lyrics of "The people have a right to know."

CHAPTER 9

Words to the Wise

Recent Scams to Avoid

Keeping current, con artists fit their swindle to the freshest topic of the day. During the lull between the First World War and Pearl Harbor, some scam artists actually went out collecting funds for the "Widow of the Unknown Soldier"! How many patriotic souls fell for that one without realizing where their donations were going?

In the early 1990s, with the Persian Gulf situation recently past, swindlers pulled out their oil-and-gas leases and gold-coin scams. With half the world worried about how to acquire fuel if the OPEC nations held petroleum hostage, buying in to oil-and-gas ventures might seem prudent. Also, when the stock market dips, gold prices usually surge; so what better commodities to peddle than black and yellow gold, even though this time gold prices dropped.

To protect themselves from confidence people, potential investors should *take it slowly* and *ask for brochures* that can be checked over by their own accountants or brokers. Swindlers usually try to rush sales and force their victims to react immediately. Most legitimate salespeople will allow potential customers time to think things over and look into them before leaping.

Travel Fraud

Travel fraud became quite popular in the late-1980s and early 1990s. Swindlers telephone victims at random or from a list of likely travelers and offer a free trip to some exotic location. The smooth-taking caller offers a simple explanation for the gift: 1) Someone in the household filled out a winning sweepstake ticket (who can remember which ones they sent in?), or 2) The family's name was picked at random from the local phone directory, or 3) The offer is a promotional gimmick to acquaint people with a particular airline or cruise line or tour, or 4) The family is being offered membership in a below-cost travel club.

Whatever the ruse, the sole aim of the call is to pry the victims' credit card numbers from them. The telephone solicitors, usually working "boiler rooms" with many other phone people, may not even know the scheme is a scam and that their employers are not on the up-and-up. All the people running the swindle want is to obtain credit card numbers, which they turn into cash. These scam operators have already opened merchant accounts with banks and have gained the ability to "sell" over the phone.

Once the swindlers have a sucker's credit card number, they can write up fake sales slips for as much as they feel they can get away with and collect from the bank—as if a real charge had been made. By the time the victim receives the bill for the fraudulent sale, the scam artists have blown town with several hundreds of thousands of dollars. The merchant account is closed, and the bank is left holding the bag when the victim refuses to pay on merchandise neither ordered nor received. Good rule of thumb: never give out a number if someone else initiated the call.

The Price of Forgetfulness

Another chilling phone ploy, in the wake of Alzheimer's Disease's discovery, is for a con artist to call and befriend an older person over a period of time—chatting and writing down everything that's said. Each day, while merely chewing the fat, the flimflammer asks specific questions about something the victim mentioned the day before. If, after a couple of days of exhibiting forgetfulness, a pattern of memory loss is established, the con artists strikes boldly:

"Hi, Sam. You're okay, aren't you? I mean, I never received the $25,000 you said you'd send me. Is there something wrong? Don't you want the gold coins for your grandkids?"

Embarrassed by having forgotten something so important and for jeopardizing the grandchildren's gift, the victim almost always writes down the address "again" and sends the money—or hands over a check to a messenger.

Preying on Fear

Also high on the list of sick methods of obtaining funds is to work a scam around AIDS, one of the 1990s hotter topics. Con artists peddle AIDS cures to gullible people who've tested out HIV positive, or they enlist people's financial aid in setting up clinics or hospices to help those with AIDS. Physicians point out that there is no "cure" for AIDS yet; funding for charitable works must be accompanied by a reputable statement of information.

Fake Art

Down through the centuries, forgers have duplicated works of art and sold them as originals. Until recently, victims found it difficult to tell a fake from the real thing. Some forgeries proved good enough to fool even the experts. With the advent of such analytic tools as carbon-14 dating, ultraviolet and X rays, fluoroscopy, and chemical spectoscopy for pigments, getting away with faking a master is almost impossible.

Of course, for every rule, there's an exception. Florida recently received such a flood of fake Salvador Dali paintings that the South Florida Better Business Bureau classified its latest forgery complaints as the "Hello, Dali" calls.

Kicking the Downtrodden

With the number of homeless people growing daily, crooks work on people's fears—taking small amounts from a large number of victims, since every little bit helps. Bunco artists, armed with official-looking paperwork, show up at the door of those whose names are on lists for public housing. Preying on those who have waited the longest, the con artists tell their victims they are with the housing authority and the place they've been waiting for is now available.

These low-rent vultures swoop down on their prey and take what they can—$200–$400 for "security deposit" on the new apartment and any legal papers that can be sold later, such as birth certificates. Sometimes they even drive the victims to their new home for a look, and then strand them there. One quick phone call to verify authenticity of the authority's representative would have saved the day.

Overseas Dreams

Beware of advertisements offering overseas work in exotic lands. Of course, the offer may be perfectly legal and legitimate, and the work rewarding; but if the ad asks for a deposit—look out. That cushy position in Hong Kong or Paris or Sydney might just be the figment of some con artist's imagination, with the deposit as the price tag.

900 Numbers Add Up

Parents have had enough problems with 900 phone numbers, trying to keep their kids off the line and themselves out of debtor's prison. But the hazards of the 900 lines run far beyond children hearing something they shouldn't at the parents' expense. Some 900 numbers are pure scam, with big damages adding up so innocently. One of the most recent swindles offers people credit. Those who have been turned down by everyone else are guaranteed credit by calling the 900 number and answering a few questions. No one will be turned down. Of course not—that's not the point.

Joe calls 907-EZ-CREDIT and hits a recording telling him that all the lines are busy and the first available operator will be right with him, and he's treated to music while he waits. Never does it dawn on him that from the moment the call was answered by the machine, he was being charged up to $15 per minute for the call.

Finally, after many musical minutes—at $15 per minute—a cheery person comes on the line and asks the normal questions to fill out the application. "Name?" "Joe Blow." "Is that Joe with an E or Jo without an E?" "With an E." "Could you spell your last name, please?" "B-l-o-w." "Is that B for boy or P for ploy?" "It's B for boy."

The caller usually answers all the questions patiently, and if there is a problem, the young person on the other end giggles and makes a joke of being new on the job—anything to keep the victim from realizing that the meter is running.

The caller will receive the credit card, which will be good only if he puts up money to cover the amount of credit he wants. But the 900 number's real function was to keep Joe Blow on the line as long as possible and to collect $15 per minute from the phone company for the call, leaving Mr. Blow to blow his stack when he gets the phone bill.

Bottom Line

If it's too good to be true—let it alone. And protect your numbers; they're all you have. Never give out your credit card numbers, your Social Security number, your birth date, or your bank account numbers to anyone who calls you. Of course, if you call a company or an ad on TV or in a magazine and want to order something, go right ahead. If you can make the purchase without giving out your number, all the better.

On the other hand, if you find yourself chatting with someone you don't know—watch out. In conversation, you might give away more than you planned and find yourself robbed of your bank account. All someone needs to have access to your accounts are the account number—which is on every check you write—and your mother's maiden name. Of course, you say, you'd never be dumb enough to tell anyone your mother's maiden name.

No, but you might fall for an interesting conversation: "Madison, that's a good old American name. Did your father's family come over on the *Mayflower*?"

"Far from it—my dad's kin were all horse thieves."

"I know what you mean. Mine, too. My dad's a Rochester—all bums. But my mother's folks, the Jeffersons—now they date way back. In fact, my mother belongs to the DAR. How about yours?"

"No, I don't think the Whitneys go back that far."

Gottcha!

Bibliography

"Accused of Fraud, Milli Vanilli Sings the Blues (or Hires Someone to Do It)." *People Weekly*, December 3, 1990, 197.

Adams, Stanley E. "S&Ls: The Final Frontier." *Harper's*, October 1990, 22–24.

Adler, Jerry, with Ginny Carroll. "Jim and Tammy Rise Again." *Newsweek*, October 19, 1987, 77.

Akst, Daniel. "How Barry Minkow Fooled the Auditors." *Forbes*, October 2, 1989, 126–132.

Aldington, Richard. *Frauds*. London: William Heinemann, Ltd., 1957.

Allen, Mel. "The Man Who Broke North Haven's Heart." *Yankee*, September 1989, 52–57.

Anderson, Ian. "Himalayan Scandal Rocks Indian Science." *New Scientist*, February 9, 1991, 17.

Ballen, Kate. "The Most Corrupt Person." *Fortune*, August 17, 1987, 93.

Best, Patricia. "Downfall of a Schemer." *Maclean's*, July 20, 1987, 32.

Blauner, Peter. "The Dream Broker." *New York*, February 11, 1985, 22–23.

Brand, David. "It Was too Good to Be True." *Time*, June 1, 1987, 59.

"California Firms, Employees Indicted on Fraud Charges." *Aviation Week & Space Technology*, April 4, 1988, 31.

Callum, Myles. "Pranks a Lot!" *TV Guide*, July 29, 1989, 23.

Castro, Janice. "Judging the Hoax That Failed." *Time*, February 25, 1985, 60.

Collingwood, Harris. "A Texas Tycoon's Tragic End." *BusinessWeek*, July 18, 1988, 82.

"Conodonts and Conan Doyle." *Economist*, April 29, 1989, 88.

Coughlin, Ellen K. " 'Avalanche' of Misinformation on Himalayan Fossils Is Attributed to Geologist at Indian University." *Chronicle of Higher Education*, April 26, 1989, A4, A6.

Crichton, Robert. *The Great Impostor*. New York: Random House, 1959.

Crudele, John. "The Big Chill." *New York*, August 24, 1987, 19–21.

Culliton, Barbara J. "A Bitter Battle over Error (II)." *Science*, July 1, 1988, 18–21.

———. "Integrity of Research Papers Questioned." *Science*, January, 1987, 422–423.

"Defrocking a Fraud." *Time*, September 28, 1987.

DeLorean, John Z. *DeLorean*. Grand Rapids, Michigan: Zondervan Books, 1984.

Dentzer, Susan, with Carolyn Friday and Elaine Shannon. "The Nightmare at Hutton." *Newsweek*, July 22, 1985, 45.

Di Landro, Mary. "Going Nowhere Fast?" *Travel-Holiday*, September, 1988, 36–38.

Dilnot, George. *Getting Rich Quick*. London: Geoffrey Bles, 1935.

Dornheim, Michael A. "Rockwell, Two Former Managers Charged with Navstar Fraud." *Aviation Week & Space Technology*, February 1, 1988, 30.

Duffy, Thom. "Milli Vanilli Didn't Start the Fire." *Billboard*, December 8, 1990, 4, 89.

Dwyer, Paula. "The Pentagon's Fraud Squad Bags a Highflier." *BusinessWeek*, September 26, 1988, 46.

Ellison, E. Jerome, and Frank W. Brock. *The Run for Your Money*. Ossining, New York: Dodge Publishing Company, 1935.

Fanning, Deidre. "The Stranger in the Corner." *Forbes*, October 5, 1987, 37–38.

Fay, Stephen, Lewis Chester, and Magnus Linklater. *Hoax*. New York: The Viking Press, 1972.

"Follow-ups." *The Nation*, January 17, 1987, 37.

"Friends Divided over the Truth." *Christianity Today*, February 19, 1990, 38.

Friedman, Jack, et al. "Victims of The Church of Love Were Only the Lonely." *People*, December 1988, 77–80.

Garfield, Eugene and Alfred Welljams-Dorof. "The Impact of Fraudulent Research on the Scientific Literature." *Journal of the American Medical Association*, March 9, 1990, 1424–1426.

"Get-Rich-Quick Deal Just a Pot of Mold." *Newsweek*, August 19, 1985, 52.

Goodman, Mark, and Sarah Skolnik. "Bright and Athletic, He Seemed Perfect for Princeton, But This Paper Tiger's Stripes Came from the Jailhouse." *People Weekly*, March 18, 1991, 74–76.

Green, Michelle. "A Social-Climbing Stockbroker Gets Pinched for Fleecing the Elite of Richmond." *People Weekly*, July 28, 1986, 67–68.

Greenwald, John. "Cutting the Deal of His Life." *Time*, April 30, 1990, 71.

"Grief for the Coroner." *Time*, August 15, 1988, 21.

Grossman, John. *Health*, October, 1986, 68–69.

Harrison, Barbara Grizzuti. "The Buck Stops Here." *Savvy*, October 1989, 68–69.

———. "The Great Talk-Show Hoax." *Mademoiselle*, January 1989, 62.

Holden, Constance. "Yale Takes Action Against Psychiatrists for Financial Improprieties." *News & Comment*, November 6, 1987, 745.

———. "Fraud Reimbursement." *Science*, September 1987, 1563.

———. "NIMH Finds a Case of 'Serious Misconduct.'" *Science*, March 1987, 1566–1567.

Hughes, Robert. "Brilliant, But Not for Real." *Time*, May 7, 1990, 118–119.

Irving, Clifford. *Fake!* New York: McGraw-Hill Book Company, 1969.

"It's Time to Jail Penny-Stock Crooks." *BusinessWeek*, November 20, 1989, 156.

Ivey, Mark, with Joseph Weber and Gary Weiss. "Turning up the Heat on a Penny-Stock Kingpin." *BusinessWeek*. May 16, 1988, 100–101.

Kasindorf, Jeanie. "Leona and Harry: Money and Love." *New York*, October 3, 1988, 40–49.

———. "Six Degrees of Impersonation." *New York*, March 25, 1991, 40–46.

Klein, Alexander. *Grand Deception*. New York: Lippincott, 1955.

Lamar, Jacob V., Jr. "Out of Africa: Stung by a Ghanaian Smoothy." *Time*, April 21, 1986, 34–35.

Lappen, Alyssa A. "The Eternal Promoter." *Forbes*, August 10, 1987, 8.

Larsen, Egon. *The Deceivers*. London: John Baker, 1966.

"Last Frontier." *The New Yorker*, February 5, 1990, 34–35.

Lewin, Roger. "The Case of the 'Misplaced' Fossils." *Science*, April 21, 1982, 277–279.

MacDonald, Craig. "Famous California Scientist Who Didn't Exist." *Fedco Reporter*, June 1991.

MacDonald, John C.R. *Crime Is a Business.* Stanford University, California: Stanford University Press, 1939.

Martz, Larry, with Kenneth L. Woodward, et al. "Gospelgate II: Target Falwell." *Newsweek,* June 1, 1987, 56–59.

Marx, Linda. "Jim and Tammy Faye Bakker Cry Hallelujah at the Chance His Prison Time Will Be Cut." *People Weekly,* 40–41.

McClintick, David. *Indecent Exposure: A True Story of Hollywood and Wall Street.* New York: William Morrow, 1982.

McKelway, St. Clair. *The Big Little Man from Brooklyn.* Boston: Houghton Mifflin Company, 1969.

"Milking Milken." *National Review,* March 18, 1991, 17–18.

Nash, Jay Robert. *Hustlers and Con Men.* New York: M. Evans, 1976.

O'Connor, Colleen, with Peter McKillop. "The Big Apple Is Beset by Rotten Apples." *Newsweek,* March 30, 1987, 30.

Oliwenstein, Lori. "Fossil Fraud." *Discover,* January 1990, 43–44.

"Ponzi Is Gone but His Game Goes On." *U.S. News & World Report,* June 10, 1985, 14.

Radolf, Andrew. "Hoaxer Strikes Again." *Editor & Publisher*, January 13, 1990, 15, 19.

Reid, Calvin. "Jury Awards $3.5 Million in Damages against Press." *Publishers Weekly*, April 20, 1990, 18.

———. "Suit Against *Fatal Vision* Author Is Settled Out of Court." *Publishers Weekly*, December 11, 1987, 12.

"The Ripoff Repertoire." *Modern Maturity*, April-May 1991, 46–47.

Roman, Mark B. "When Good Scientists Turn Bad." *Discover*, April, 1988, 51–58.

Rose, Colin, ed. *The World's Greatest Rip-Offs*. New York: Sterling Publishing Company, 1978.

Russell, Deborah. "Grammy Whammy: Milli Vanilli Sings the Blues (Honest)." *Billboard*, December 1, 1990, 1, 81.

Satterfield, David. "A Nice Local Boy but a Swindler." *50 Plus*, June, 1988, 17.

"Scam Lines." *Harper's Magazine*, November, 1987, 15–17.

Schwartz, John. "Take the Money and Sink." *Newsweek*, March 5, 1990, 34.

Scott, Debra. "The Maidstone Scam." *New York*, September 23, 1985, 72–82.

Shipman, Pat. "On the Trail of the Piltdown Fraudsters." *New Scientist*, October 6, 1990, 52–54.

Stoker, Bram. *Famous Impostors*. New York: Sturgis & Walton Company, 1910.

Vallance, Aylmer. *Very Private Enterprise*. London: Thames and Hudson, 1955.

Wadler, Joyce. "His Story Is a Big Hit on Broadway, but This Con Man Is in Trouble Again." *People Weekly*, March 18, 1991, 99–100.

Waggoner, Dianna. "A British Con Man Says the Devil Made Him Do It." *People Weekly*, June 16, 1986, 119–120.

Welles, Chris. "The Drexel Affair: A Shoe Finally Drops." *BusinessWeek*, June 20, 1988, 46.

Wilentz, Amy. "A Latter-Day Forger." *Time*, February 2, 1987, 32.

Willoughby, Jack. "A License to Steal." *Forbes*, September 22, 1986, 146–148.

Zuckerman, Solly. "A New Clue to the Real Piltdown Forger?" *New Scientist*, November 3, 1990, 16.